WRITING MYSTERIES

A HANDBOOK BY THE
MYSTERY WRITERS OF AMERICA

WRITING MYSTERIES

A HANDBOOK BY THE MYSTERY WRITERS OF AMERICA

EDITED BY SUE GRAFTON

Writer's
Digest
Books

Cincinnati, Ohio

96 95 94 93 92   5 4 3 2 1

Library of Congress Cataloging-in-Publication Data

Writing mysteries : a handbook / by the Mystery Writers of America :
    Sue Grafton, editor. — 1st ed.
        p.   cm.
    Includes bibliographical references (p.   ) and index.
    ISBN 0-89879-502-8
    1. Detective and mystery stories — Authorship.   I. Grafton, Sue.
II. Mystery Writers of America.
PN3377.5.D4W66   1992
808.3'872 — dc20   91-34403
                                                                        CIP

Designed by Carol Buchanan

For permissions information see pages 207 and 208.

A Word of Thanks From the Editor ...

Had space permitted, there are many other writers whose views I would have loved to include in this handbook. Unfortunately, the limitations of length and scope were such that not all of my favorites could be represented. Some writers I approached were forced to decline from press of other work. Most did so with a graciousness that left no doubt about their affection for the genre.

Throughout the process of preparing this edition for publication, I was always conscious of the inestimable donation of time, energy and expertise each writer was being asked to contribute. The modest honorarium permitted by the budget came nowhere near compensating these professionals for their generosity.

And finally . . .

Since the predecessor of this handbook (*The Mystery Writer's Handbook*, Writer's Digest Books) was published, some of the masters left us: Agatha Christie, James M. Cain, John Dickson Carr, Ross MacDonald, Daphne du Maurier, John D. Macdonald, Georges Simenon, Ngaio Marsh and Rex Stout. We can never adequately acknowledge their gifts to us. Because of their achievements, and the continued dedication of those of us still writing, the mystery will live on.

Sue Grafton
Santa Barbara, California

CONTENTS

PART II THE PROCESS
THE BEGINNING

PART III SPECIALTIES

ABOUT THE EDITOR

Sue Grafton has written novels, articles, short fiction, a screenplay and numerous teleplays. She has also lectured on writing at colleges and conferences in Southern California and the Midwest. Her first mystery, *A is for Alibi*, won an award from the Cloak and Clue Society of Wisconsin. *B is for Burglar* won both the Anthony Award and the Shamus Award for best novel of 1985, and *C is for Corpse* won the Anthony Award for best novel in 1986. "The Parker Shotgun" won a Macavity Award from the Mystery Readers of America and an Anthony for Best Short Story of 1986. She has also won the Mystery Guild Award for best hardcover novel three years in a row. Sue Grafton's father, C.W. Grafton, is also a mystery writer, and she credits much of her affection for the form to her father.

Grafton, who was born in Louisville, Kentucky, now lives in Southern California with her husband, Steven Humphrey.

FOREWORD

If you're approaching the mystery for the first time, you may not yet appreciate the profound mastery of the form required to succeed. If you've already written your first mystery (even your second or third), you'll know just how exasperating, exhilarating, rewarding, frustrating and satisfying the genre can be. What we've done here is assemble some of the finest writers working in the field, describing with humor and candor the means and methods each has devised in tackling the mystery-writing process.

The creation of complex and believable characters is essential to the writing of a successful mystery. Whether it's a short story or a full-length novel, the narrative line needs to be strong, the prose style crisp, the pace relentless. But there are many other elements to conquer beyond the basics of character and plot. A mystery is more than a novel, more than a compelling account of people whose fate engages us. The mystery is a way of examining the dark side of human nature, a means by which we can explore, vicariously, the perplexing questions of crime, guilt and innocence, violence and justice. The mystery not only re-creates the original conditions from which violence springs, tracking the chaos that murder unleashes, but then attempts to divine the truth through the process of rational investigation and eventually restores an order to the universe.

That's a bit much, you may complain. How can you, as a mystery writer, accomplish such an impossible feat? You must become, first and foremost, a student of human nature, a self-appointed armchair psychologist, willing not only to analyze and understand your fellow creatures, but to inquire into your own soul and chart its contradictions. Translating your insights into fiction isn't easy, but the mystery is the perfect vehicle for the observations you have made. The term *mystery* is an umbrella that shelters a variety of subgenres: the traditional whodunit, the private eye, the classic puzzle, the police procedural, action/adventure, thriller, espionage, the novels of psychological and romantic suspense. You would do well to consider the assets and the drawbacks of each before you decide which is best suited for the particular story you wish to tell.

In addition to pace and suspense, there are questions of tone and atmosphere, the use of description, the balance of action, exposition and dialogue. There are also requirements peculiar to the genre: clues, and red herrings, the tying up of loose ends. As a mystery writer, you will need to acquire at least a nodding acquaintance with technical matters such as forensics, ballistics and police procedure. We are, after all, writing about murder, which involves a number of specialists whose job it is to address the scientific and legal aspects of the subject. While you may not have to be a licensed expert yourself, you may be writing *about* the experts and you'll need to know enough about a given subject to convey both data and attitudes convincingly. A mystery writer needs to have an understanding of how the judicial system works, a knowledge of investigative procedures, access to specialized information, both mundane and exotic.

Aside from their technical proficiency, mystery writers are the magicians of fiction. We're the illusionists, working with sleight of hand in the performance of our art. With this book, we'll be taking you behind the scenes so you can see how the riddles are created and the illusions sustained. Keep in mind that the mystery is the one form in which the reader and the writer are pitted against each other. Your job, as a practicing mystery writer, is to lay out a believable tale of intrigue and ingenuity . . . always with the proviso that you play fair with the reader, who in turn will be doing his or her best to catch you at your tricks. You would do well, incidentally, to assume your reader is at least as smart as you.

We've designed this book as a walk-through, taking you from the first flash of inspiration to the point at which you'll search for an agent or an editor, finished manuscript in hand. Every work of fiction you write begins with an idea, sometimes quite fleeting, which you must work to develop, fleshing out the bare bones of theme and plot, layering in characters, making a hundred decisions about setting, tone, point of view, the style appropriate to the story you want to tell. As you progress through the book, you'll find suggestions about ways to research, approaches to character and plotting, techniques for outlining the story as it takes shape. You'll find advice about dialogue, about planting clues and building suspense. From beginning, to middle, to the rousing climax of your book, we're here, like an army of experts, to offer guidance and assistance. We'll even counsel you about stumbling blocks, what most writers think of as the three-quarter mark sag, advising you what to do when you lose steam momentarily and the book sags under its own weight.

You'll hear many distinct points of view expressed here, but you'll also find many areas where our attitudes merge. It's been said that to learn something new, you need to hear it three times. You'll note the dictum at work here. Some points about the mystery are made over and over again from the perspective of writers whose work may appear very different on the surface. We've allowed the repetitions to remain, hoping you'll take comfort from the fact that so many of us agree on the basics.

The truth of the matter is that you must teach yourself how to write. We can offer guidance, the painful wisdom of our own hard won experience, but in the end, you must hone your own skills, conquering the countless devils that will plague you as you learn. As a mystery writer, you will have to serve a long and sometimes arduous apprenticeship. We offer encouragement, our own excitement at the prospect.

This, then, is our gift to you.

While the journey is yours, we offer you this road map. We warn you of the pitfalls. We point you toward the high ground.

As working members of The Mystery Writers of America, we wish you Godspeed.

Sue Grafton

INTRODUCTION

Gregory Mcdonald

A novel to be novel must be novel.

Frequently things most simply stated are the most difficult to do.

As with any other invention, the novel, the short story, ideally ought *do* something never done before.

The five W's are taught to anyone wishing to write. Regarding any story, you are taught you must report the Who, What, Where, When and Why.

Before you ever think seriously of writing creatively, for your own sake, you must establish, as much as humanly possible, the Who, What, Where, When and Why of yourself.

You are the only source of your originality, and the only person who can develop the skill to make that originality of interest or value to others.

Too often have I heard a writer, an agent, editor, publisher, critic say, "Such and such book is great. It's just like such and such book."

I yawn.

What I need to hear is that such and such novel, story, is *unlike* anything I've ever read before, has some new element in it, something truly creative, original enough to justify its existence, and to arouse my interest in it.

The creative process starts with your establishing in your own mind what new element uniquely, personally *you*, you are going to bring to the short story, the novel, particularly *your* short story, *your* novel. Creative work is much too difficult to launch into blindly, without having a truly novel idea, and *without knowing as precisely and as consciously as possible what that idea is.*

That accomplished is the good beginning that makes your work half done.

So you have a novel idea.

A mathematics teacher, Dr. Raymond Dwinnell Farnsworth, used to point out to his young charges, myself among them, that we wouldn't build a doghouse without first recognizing the function of what we are about to build (a house for a dog; a small dog? a medium-sized dog? a large dog?), researching the project, drawing up a detailed plan, gathering the necessary materials and tools, knowing where we are going to put the doghouse once finished, etc. "How is it," he would ask, "people so often think they can solve an intellectual, creative problem without first establishing a plan, a method, doing the things they would do automatically when planning to build a doghouse?"

I expect you've had the same experience as I of coming across people who, in their professional or personal lives, have spent time, money, energy or other precious resources only to find themselves blocked, failing, having to abandon the effort, simply because they had not a clear idea of what they intended from the very beginning.

Especially can the writer save himself massive amounts of grief, thousands of hours of work, an enormous consumption of mental, physical, emotional energy, utter failure, simply by establishing in his own mind what a work is to *do*.

Is your work going to entertain people, inform them, instruct them, intrigue them, improve them, make them laugh, cry, what?

Only you know.

If you are working in fiction, it is recommended your first answer is that you are going to use the idea *to tell a story*.

It's an old saw that there really are something like only twenty-seven basic plots humans have discovered so far. The number changes up and down, but tomes have been written on this contention.

Plots are believed to be limited.

The mystery is perhaps the most explicit of all plots. As with any writing, you pose the question in the beginning, as quickly as possible, and by the end have answered the question as satisfactorily as possible. The question posed in the mystery form is right on the surface of the work, impossible to miss, *Who done what?*

Purists insist the mystery must be confined to all conceivable variations within the basic, explicit puzzle plot. A strong, even poetic sense of place may be given. Class criticism, rather than social comment, traditionally is permissible. Yet humor, wit other than the ironic, is not seen as desirable to the pure mystery. And romance, love, sex, especially for the protagonist, except as a cool, objective plot element, definitely is frowned upon as intrusive.

This is a respectable point of view.

However, it is also mathematically a most constricting point of view.

Geniuses of generations prior to this last explored and exploited this highly constrictive form of the pure mystery to a great and wonderful extent. A few still work within it, some with great success. So well explored was the pure mystery form that at the beginning of this last generation, the mystery, especially as a written form, was dying. It was being considered an art form that had peaked in the 1920s, 1930s, 1940s.

Mathematics, upon which all art is based, permits, if not the concept of the infinite, at least the concept of the indefinite.

Personally, I abhor labeling, categorizing, anything that constricts any art form. Only those rules that are continuously tested deserve to stand.

When people ask me why I write mysteries, I answer, "Because it lets me get away with murder."

To me, the mystery form provides that line of suspense provided by the question *Who done what?*, stout enough to hang from it ideas sometimes too heavy for more precious forms, of similar length.

Today, before you start writing your mystery, you are more free, you have far wider (and deeper) choices to make.

I have been amazed when I have heard mystery writers I love and admire say they will twist the characters to fit the plot but never twist the plot to fit the characters.

To me, mathematically again, this does not make sense.

Plots, as stated, are believed limited.

Characters are limitless.

Thus my advice always is to start with the characters.

To my mind, *everything*, the story, the wit, the comment, the theme, all comes from the energy, the electricity of putting the right characters together, at the right time, in the right place.

Do you choose an ordinary character who finds himself in extraordinary circumstances?

Or do you choose an extraordinary character in ordinary circumstances?

Thus a good, wide beginning in your effort to establish the original, the novel, is in your creation of a character, characters.

And how do you do that? How do you create a character?

I doubt there's any one answer. Tom Betancourt (*Running Scared*) is an *idea*, a reflection of his society. Fletch is the embodiment of the spirit not only of his time, postrevolutionary, late twentieth-century American, "the barefoot boy with cheek," but also of the blithe spirit of journalism about whom I had been hearing tales since I was a twinkle. Robby Burnes (*Safekeeping*) clearly is a foil; Thadeus Lowry a composite of many I had known. With the line, "Pardon my pants. I'm fresh from an axe murder," Flynn stepped suddenly and unexpectedly full blown from the page. Instantly he was a character who needed to be explored through three novels of his own.

One thing is certain: You must have an empathic understanding of your character; an equatorial citizen who has never been cold obviously would find it difficult, if not impossible, to write convincingly of a citizen of Antarctica.

Never directly, deliberately have I written as a fictional character someone I have known. I don't believe it fair. We have only our *perceptions* of people, no absolute knowledge of how people really are. And it isn't wise. After decades of believing you know someone well sometimes you can discover your perceptions of that someone totally wrong (as I did once, in discovering someone I had known a generation had been living all that time what can only be called a double life).

Some authors write only one character well, and that character frequently is the author's superego.

I prefer the multiphrenic author: each character he writes develops from his own experience, character and empathy. I am as much Chump Hardy as I am David MacFarlane as I am Dan Prescott as I am John Bart Nelson (*Time Squared*[2]). Yet notice that although I wrote from each of these male's point of view, and that I have written *of* women, such as Ms. Tuesday in the same work, I discovered some time ago, I cannot write *from* the woman's point of view. *I do not know what a woman does when she is in a room alone.*

The characters you develop depend upon who *you* are.

Hemingway was Hemingway.

Shakespeare was everyone else.

There are only two places to set a story: the world that you physically know or can re-create through historic research, or Prospero's island in Shakespeare's *The Tempest*: a world of your own creation, which is everywhere and nowhere simultaneously.

The grief about writing is that people generally start because they feel they have something to say. It takes so long to learn the craft that frequently after people have learned the craft they discover they no longer have anything to say.

Learning the craft of art too often knocks the essential child out of the artist.

A cartoonist friend, Al Ferguson, once sat on my porch and discussed elephants. To an adult, he said, an elephant is an elephant, a big, gray, animate thing, with a trunk at one end and a tail at the other. To a scientist, a reporter, an elephant is something so many feet tall, so many feet long, so many pounds heavy. To a child an elephant is Wow! The artist, Al said, is an adult/scientist/reporter who has never lost his *Wow!* view of the elephant, of life, of the world.

To me, writing is not a job, a vocation, an avocation: it is a response to life. A response, which, unfortunately, requires the deliberate, hard development of a craft. I suspect one is only willing to go through the duress of learning such a difficult craft because one is motivated, empowered by the belief that one has something to say, to contribute. How many policemen, how many surgeons have you known whose entire personalities have been changed by their experiences in learning their craft?

As you study the clues on writing in this handbook and other works on writing, as you take your courses, gather your experiences, and write your journals, your poems and stories and novels, do not forget why you are doing this. Do not lose yourself. Keep yourself. Keep your ideas. You are developing your craft for one reason and one reason alone: so that ultimately you can contribute to the world that original, telling, showing, *novel* view of the world, existence that can only come from you.

Before you start any writing, before you learn the craft, before you begin making your choices regarding what form your ideas will take, first you must know yourself. Your ideas will mature with time. And as you learn your craft, you will come to express your ideas with increasing effectiveness.

Never forget that craft without originality is not art.

And that you, not this book or any other, not this teacher or that admired writer, that you, and only you, are the sole source of any originality available to you.

PART 1

PREPARATION

CHAPTER 1

THE RULES AND HOW TO *BEND* THEM

JERMIAH HEALY

When Sue Grafton asked me to write this article, she suggested as a title "The Rules and How to *Break* Them." Now, being both an attorney and a law professor, I naturally never break a rule. I have learned, however, that there are times when an old rule should be abandoned or a current rule should not be applied. In other words, the rule should be *bent*, usually because the reason behind the rule — the reason the rule was originally imposed — wouldn't be promoted by adhering to the rule.

For example, most states say that confidential communications between spouses are privileged from disclosure. What's the reason behind such a rule? Probably, the jurisdiction wants to encourage the exchange of intimacies that promotes a marriage relationship. However, if the wife has sued the husband for divorce, then at least communications thereafter should not be privileged, even though the couple is still technically "married." Why? Because the reason behind the rule just no longer applies. One spouse's filing for divorce shows that there is no longer a marriage relationship to promote.

Let me take a similar approach to the "rules" of mystery writing. I will focus on the rules that supposedly govern the private investigator novel, suggesting the reason(s) behind each and where you can do some bending. Since most of us are aware of the Ten Commandments, let me follow that pattern in identifying the rules.

I. The Plot Is Everything

The first rule of mystery writing can be stated simply: The plot is everything. All other aspects of the book must be slaves to the story line. A solid reason behind this rule is that most readers come to a mystery because the genre promises an actual story, a characteristic that many find lacking in so-called mainstream fiction. Also, many readers truly want a tale in which the problem is resolved and the guilty party is punished, a disposition that is sadly lacking in many real-life bad acts. Given the reasons behind this rule, I would not try to bend it.

II. The Hero Must Be Male

The typical hero in a private investigator novel (as opposed to other types of mysteries) was a man. Why? Presumably, there was a perception that the public would accept as a private investigator only a male with certain physical strengths and acquired capabilities, like being a good shot or a tough street fighter. At first blush, this reason behind the rule wasn't completely crazy: many real-life private investigators were former law enforcement or military service personnel, professions that were almost exclusively male until relatively recently.

However, society has changed dramatically. I served with female military police officers in the 1970s, and there are now plenty of women in civilian law enforcement as street cops or investigators. Accordingly, the perception has changed, and with it, the reason behind the rule as well. Thanks to Sue Grafton, Linda Barnes and Sara Paretsky, we now have Kinsey Millhone, Carlotta Carlyle and V.I. Warshawski, respectively. This "rule" can be abandoned so long as the character, male or female, is credible.

A common aspect of the *stereo*typical private eye was that of heterosexual rogue, presumably to attract and satisfy an audience thought to aspire to that questionable status. Happily, the reason behind the rule no longer supports this aspect either. My own investigator, John Francis Cuddy, is heterosexual but not a rogue: He remains faithful to the memory of his dead wife until he meets a woman to whom he can commit. Joseph Hansen's Dave Brandstetter is neither heterosexual nor a rogue: he chooses his gay lovers carefully and stays with one for many of the books in the series. So long as the character is carefully drawn, he or she is no longer subject to expectations of preference or promiscuity.

III. The Setting Will Be Los Angeles

The classic setting for a private investigator was L.A. Historically, Raymond Chandler chose that city for Philip Marlowe. Current authors have followed that tradition (e.g., Arthur Lyons for Jacob Asch and Robert Crais for Elvis Cole). I don't believe this choice was ever a rule, especially given Dashiell Hammett's setting of San Francisco for Sam Spade. The reason behind this presumed rule was that the "city of angels" provided a variety of social classes, ethnicities and corrupt officials. With all respect, a lot of cities (and many large towns) have these advantages. Witness Marcia Muller's selection of San Francisco for Sharon McCone, Jonathan Valin's Cincinnati for Harry Stoner, Loren Estleman's Detroit for Amos Walker, Lawrence Block's New York for Matt Scudder, and Benjamin Schutz's Washington, D.C. for Leo Haggerty. The reason behind the rule of setting should be to have a place that provides a suitable backdrop for your story line and a pool of different characters for your cast. Therefore, choose your setting based on a combination of your needs and your familiarity.

IV. Some Violence Is Required

There must be some violence in a private investigator book. The reason behind this rule is that without violence our knight errant is neither tested nor confirmed in his or her physical courage. However, the trick is to make the violence rational and advance the story line. In real life, a private investigator who discharged his or her weapon (outside a firing range) three times in a year, even without hitting anybody, would surely lose the permit to carry that weapon. Accordingly, be sure your violence, particularly if committed by the hero, is proportionate to the provocation involved. Also, have your violence occur at different points of the book to pace the plot and revive the reader. If you are philosophically troubled by blood onstage, have some of your violence occur offstage.

The one mandate that the rule of violence still carries, at least for a private investigator novel, is that there must be at least one death-by-criminal-act in the book. There are some current practitioners who do not observe this rule, and frankly I come away from their work feeling unsatisfied as a reader.

V. Certain Violence Is Prohibited

The mirror image of the previous rule is that there are some types of violence that are not acceptable, even in fiction. The virtually taboo areas include graphic scenes of child abuse, rape and cruelty to animals. The reason behind this rule is common decency. I once skated close to this prohibition, having my private investigator protagonist discover a kitten flayed alive by a bad guy. I quickly received "I-had-to-stop-reading-the-book" from fans and "I-wish-you-hadn't-done-that" from booksellers. Even though the act occurred offstage and the scene advanced the plot, the rule-as-taboo was deemed broken.

VI. Write in the First-Person Narrative

Returning briefly to the gods, there is a sense that the private investigator novel must be written in the first-person narrative style rather than the third-person narrative because that's the way both Hammett and Chandler did it. By way of comeback, both Hammett and Chandler wrote detective stories in both the first- and third-person styles, so this "rule" never really was a rule. However, the reason behind it is instructive: When the narrator speaks to the reader as "I," the reader comes to identify with the narrator and accepts the limitations of information that the typically chronological progression of first-person imposes on the structure of the book.

Only a few current practitioners in the private eye field use the third-person narrative. The most successful examples are the Whistler series by Robert Campbell and the Alo Nudger series by John Lutz. Both these masters manage to engage the reader's interest and loyalty. Unless you are an accomplished writer, however, I believe that the rule of first-person narrator is a good one to follow. Just remember that what the first person giveth the first person also taketh away: All your story line development has to occur through the eyes (and therefore the restricted field of vision) of your narrator, and many great "words" would sound false coming from his or her lips (and therefore your vocabulary options become restricted as well).

VII. The Hero Cannot Be the Culprit

The rule also has a mirror image: The culprit cannot be the hero. It is particularly difficult to develop a plot in which the first-person narrator turns out to be the culprit. Also, the reader, having come to identify with the hero, feels betrayed when the person the reader trusted turns out to be the criminal. Finally, the hero as criminal is presumably someone the reader (or the potential editor) feels he or she cannot adopt as a series character. Accordingly, at least in private investigator fiction, the first-person narrator being the culprit should be avoided, unless the traitorous hero is virtually crucified at the end of the book as retribution for the betrayal of the reader.

VIII. The Culprit Must Appear Early

A rule that makes a lot of sense is that the author must introduce the culprit early. I believe that the name or label of the character who is to be the culprit should be introduced in the first few chapters, with the actual face-to-face meeting of the investigator and the culprit occurring before a third of the novel is gone. The reason behind this rule is ultimate fairness to the reader: at least part of the reason he or she is plowing through your book is a sense of solving the puzzle before the investigator, and crucial information as to each suspect — and especially the culprit — is necessary to play fair with your investigating companion.

IX. Use Only Two-Character Scenes

A rule many of us observe without stating is that each scene should involve only the protagonist detective and one other character. The reason for this is basic: The writer can alert the reader to a change of speaker simply by a change in paragraphs without annoying the reader by a lot of express signals. My favorite example of this is Robert B. Parker's Spenser books, in which the dialogue simply flows with only occasional cues of "I said" or "Susan said" for the reader who has lost his or her place.

If you need to have more than two characters populating a scene, then be sure each has a distinctive "voice" so that you don't confuse the reader by not providing express signals. Though not a "private investigator" novelist, I think Elmore Leonard is the best example of a writer who can capture a different voice without offensively caricaturing the social class or ethnicity of the character speaking.

X. Authenticity Is Required

Most writers believe in the need to be authentic. The reason behind this rule is that you do not wish to offend a "ringer" reader who knows more about the subject than you do. To expand a hypothetical I've used before, Robert Randisi and Parnell Hall have to be sure they are using the right subway lines in their books about Manhattan and Brooklyn. On the other hand, Nancy Pickard and Bill Pronzini can create credible, but fictional, towns outside Boston and San Francisco in which Main Street can run either north-south or east-west. However, none of us can afford to have a character fire seven bullets from a Smith & Wesson Combat Masterpiece without reloading. The interpretation of this rule is simple: You must be authentic when you are trying to be authentic. Accordingly, research and perhaps the help of an "expert" as proofreader is vitally important when you are dealing with real-life facts.

Conclusion

There are rules that can be bent and others that should be observed strictly. With a little thought, you can be your own lawyer in determining when the reason behind the rule permits bending or dictates adherence.

CHAPTER 2

SPARKS, TRIGGERS AND FLASHES

MARILYN WALLACE

At book signings, conferences and conventions, a mystery writer can be sure that, eventually, three things will be asked: Someone will wonder whether you use a word processor to compose, someone will inquire about your work habits, and an eager questioner will surely ask, "Where do you get your ideas?"

The replies to the first two are fairly predictable.

"I always/never/after first draft work on a computer."

"I work every morning/afternoon/evening for four/six/eight hours."

It's in response to "Where do you get your ideas?" that writers take the opportunity to be really creative. "From Cleveland/Macy's/the cosmic pipeline," the writer explains. The questioner goes away entertained but unsatisfied. The respondent worries whether glibness is the proper refuge from such a familiar query, decides brevity was the required virtue, and goes home to work on her book.

The work consists of pushing, prodding, pulling and otherwise trying to wrest a book or story from a glimmer of a notion. And while she's so engaged, she realizes that it would have been helpful to provide the answers to several more specific questions: What sparks you to write a mystery? What triggers the decision to turn an idea into a novel or a short story? If you can't start working right away, how do you keep the flash of an idea from fading away completely?

Of course, what works for one writer won't necessarily be effective for another. And what's useful today may not have the same result a month later for the same writer. Still, the questions are worth exploring.

What Sparks You to Write a Mystery?

Since mysteries deal with people in the throes of powerful emotions — greed, fury, revenge, love, lust — it helps to be attuned to those emotions in yourself and in others. What makes your blood boil? What are you desperate to protect? to gain? What makes you angry, afraid, confused? What issues or incidents most often bring you closest to hostile confrontation with other people? In what circumstances do you find yourself evading or embellishing the truth? What self-deceptions, manipulations, obsessions are part of your personal repertoire? Paying honest attention to your own feelings is one starting point of crime fiction. Since most of us will not directly experience the acts we write about, what we can do instead is be aware of our emotions and what incites them. This is a variation on the often repeated principle of writing what you know: Write what you *feel* and you're on your way.

What musings take you on extended mental journeys? For me, questions that engage my curiosity are often the starting point of fiction. "The Sentence" followed after weeks of pondering the nature of obsession. *Primary Target* came out of discussions with friends about what life would be like for the first woman to run for president of the United States.

Pay attention to those things that interest you deeply. A story infused with the writer's passion to tell it is always more engrossing. Dick Francis cares about horses; Tony Hillerman cares about Navajos; Mary Higgins Clark cares about ordinary people caught in extraordinary circumstances. Enough said?

Every pearl of mystery fiction begins with a grain of an idea that serves as an irritant.

For many writers, the fascination and, indeed, the *mystery* of human behavior is the starting point for fiction. Because we're such a mobile, gregarious society, access to other people's lives is commonplace; potential stories abound. A snatch of conversation between a mother and her adult daughter, overheard in the airport, leads you to wonder about the lives of the people you're so shamelessly eavesdropping on. Why is the daughter hissing orders at the mother? What will happen after the mother boards her plane? The direct gaze of an unshaven man dressed in tatters pierces you with the knowledge that he was once someone's son. What sequence of events robbed him of his hope?

Personally, my tolerance for lack of closure must be very low — I feel compelled to explain these things to myself, and that practice lends itself to creating fiction.

Your storytelling may be stimulated by a newspaper article that reports something unusual or intriguing. I was electrified by an article about a woman who, under hypnosis, recalled the details of a murder that she claims she saw twenty-five years earlier. What happened to bring the memory to the surface now? How will law enforcement officials react to a chain of evidence a quarter-century old? The questions and images generated by reading about this case may take years to work their way toward fictional life, but I can tell by my visceral response that I'll eventually use it in some way.

Susan Dunlap says that when she's writing her Jill Smith series, all she has to do is sit back and read the local papers about Berkeley, California. The town, she admits, provides her with endless material. Of course, if you've chosen a city less colorful than Berkeley, you may have to work a little harder to identify its fiction-provoking qualities. Look for the conflicts inherent in the social, political and economic life of a region, and you may find a starting point for a mystery.

When Mickey Friedman was interviewed by Carolyn Wheat at a writers' breakfast, she revealed that hot climates intrigue her. Her face became transformed as she spoke of the decadence, the decay, the *slime* of Venice, Florida, India, the south of France — all places she's captured wonderfully in her mysteries. Some places are so thoroughly imbued with menace, either blatantly (mean streets, moody moors) or in contrast to an idyllic patina (cozy villages, relaxed resorts) that a writer's imagination is stirred into action. Novels of suspense, particularly those with ties to the gothic tradition, rely heavily on such laden settings. Watch for places that excite strong responses in you.

Most writers are also incurable readers. Intriguing facts, gleaned from eclectic reading, can push buttons. Did you know that a suicide who wears glasses almost always takes them off before jumping to his death? What if a jumper is found splattered on the sidewalk . . . still wearing his glasses? Scientific oddities, historical trivia, or even unusual psychological or spiritual systems can spark the beginning of an idea.

Wherever you find that initial inspiration, learn not to censor yourself too early in the writing process. Something that at first glance seems to be a cliché can be given a spin that will take it out of the realm of the ordinary, while an idea or an image that seems too strange even for fiction can often be tamed into usefulness. Sticking too close to the origins of an idea can keep you from seeing its dramatic possibilities. Allow your mind to play awhile; see what catches fire, what continues to simmer, and what turns to cold gray ash.

What Triggers the Decision to Turn an Idea Into a Novel or a Short Story?

The answer to this is very nearly straightforward.

If a trick ending, a gimmick or a title presents itself first, or if you've imagined a moment in which a character says "AHA!" it's likely that the idea is best suited to be a short story. A gimmick hardly has the heft to carry the burdens of character and plot development required in a novel. On the other hand, the impact of a punch ending, along with Poe's "unity of effect," are hallmarks of the mystery or suspense short story.

"A Tale of Two Pretties," began its fictional life as a title that popped into my head when I wasn't looking. It tickled me and I got to thinking about Dickens and the noble melodrama of Sidney Carton and Charles Darnay. And suddenly, from a title that appeared unbidden, I was working on a short story in which two women decide that the way out of their personal problems is to trade places.

If, on the other hand, you're intrigued by a relationship or a moral dilemma or a social situation, it's clear that you need the larger canvas of a novel on which to explore. A vague idea, unformed but seductive, has potential for development as a novel. In the next stages of work, the themes will emerge and the plot and characters take shape, but sometimes that can't happen until your initial idea has a companion.

You may be one of those people for whom it takes at least two major ideas to make a novel. When something gnaws at you and refuses to go away, even though you can't figure out how to use it, don't discard it. It might just be waiting for a complementary piece to make it workable. It's not always predictable when and how those lone notions will match up. But at some point, the two parts become interwoven and take on a shape that's not one or the other but a third, new configuration.

My first novel, *A Case of Loyalties*, provided me with the inkling that mystery fiction might work this way. A painter-friend who lives in a small town about three hours north of New York City called one day and told me that her sixteen-year-old daughter had just been arrested for stealing a car. I listened to her concerns, her frustration, her anger, her desire to do the right parental thing, and it struck deep emotional chords in me.

That was the first thread.

Four days later, a painter-friend who lives in Oakland, California, called to talk about the drive-by shooting she'd seen from her apartment window.

The two threads began to intertwine. Perhaps the proximity in time and the fact that they both involved painters and cars led to this merging. But then the story developed a life of its own. The painter-mother in the book is neither of my friends, and yet she's both of them. The fictional events don't resemble their sources except in the most superficial terms. But it still took both threads for that novel to happen; it grew from my emotional connection to both situations.

Deciding the most appropriate form is only one of the decisions you face after you have that first idea. In fact, growing a novel is much like doing an acrostic puzzle. You start with a character or a place or a fact or a situation, and eventually, by a back-and-forth process, you fit in all the pieces that weren't part of your generating spark. You ask: What if? What next? Why this? Sooner or later, you know what really happened and you know what appears to have happened. You make decisions about how the truth will be revealed. From one step to the next, especially when you're writing a novel, the original idea may become so transformed that you're surprised to see where it's all led.

For me, that's part of the excitement of writing.

If You Can't Start Working Right Away, How Do You Keep the Flash of an Idea From Fading Away Completely?

Suppose you're one of those writers constantly assaulted by glimmers of ideas. "So many ideas, so little time," is your lament. Perhaps you're already writing a mystery and you're so afraid of losing a hot new concept that you're tempted to start writing another book before you've finished the one you're already working on. (All you can learn from this process is how to *start* a book. Besides, I haven't seen any half-books in my local bookstores lately.) Maybe you're inundated by the work that's paying your bills until you can "quit your day job." How do you hold onto ideas that seem exciting until you're ready to work on them?

Some writers say that the measure of a good idea is its ability to survive without being written down. A bad idea, they contend, will slip into the murky depths of memory unretrieved and die a well-deserved death. But if you've accumulated so many tidbits of data (the telephone numbers of your three best sixth-grade friends, all the words to the Grateful Dead's "Ripple," the names of all the bones in your foot) that things are getting crowded in your brain, you may not feel very secure about being able to recall an unformed idea a year later.

Write down those elusive wisps of ideas. Write down a key phrase or a twenty-page outline but commit the thought to paper. It may lie in the bottom of a drawer and, mercifully, never rise above the underlayers. One of these long-forgotten notes may become the key to a scene, or a story, or even a novel. The physical act of writing something down will reinforce it in your mind and the idea will gain legitimacy so that you'll be better able to remember its existence. Even if you never find the piece of paper, having written it down will fix it more firmly in your mind. Something to do with a writer's wiring, I suppose, but I'm not especially concerned with explaining it. I just know it works!

Gillian Roberts goes a step further when she suggests storing characters who interest you in an imaginary apartment house. Diabolically efficient — the characters will bring their individual conflicts to this new community and will begin to interact and perhaps may even develop stories on their own.

Two Final Caveats

First, don't talk your ideas to death. This is a hard lesson to learn, but you soon discover how quickly the need to create fiction fizzles after you've told the plot of your new novel to the fourth or fifth friend who has the patience to listen. If you don't altogether kill it, the desire to write it may become so diluted that it's hard to get your storytelling juices going again.

And, especially, don't ever be afraid of running out of ideas. I promise you, more will come.

Mysteries have an enduring appeal because they tell a story of people and passions, conflicts and consequences; they chronicle the moral dilemmas and interpersonal collisions of our times. And since change is one of the constants of our world, you can be sure that new collisions and fresh dilemmas will continue to arise to spark your imagination, trigger your desire to tell a story, and ignite your flash of inspiration.

Chapter 3

On Work Schedules

Dick Lochte

Every writer has to have some sort of work schedule, even those who don't actually do any writing. These nonwriting writers busy themselves with their real occupations, usually something that keeps them firmly in the public eye — like repeating an author's lines every night on stage, or appearing on television in a three-story tic-tac-toe construction. They have definite schedules that they shift imperceptibly to include infrequent meetings with the ghosts who are putting their thoughts on paper, or with the publicists who are arranging for their media appearances to promote the books that they haven't written. We can learn nothing from the work habits of those nonpractitioners of the art.

And, to tell the truth, I'm not sure that there is much more to be gleaned from the specific habits of genuine practitioners, since the systems one uses to create a work of fiction are as individual as one's taste in clothes.

Take the great Raymond Chandler, for example. I seem to recall that in one of his collected letters he described a rather Spartan technique for forging ahead on his novels. He would set a number of hours aside each day in which, while he did not force himself to write, he refused to allow himself the pleasure of doing anything else. He just sat there in his room. Since he completed only six novels in twenty years, it follows that he spent a ghastly amount of time staring at blank walls and even blanker sheets of paper. No wonder he wound up hitting the sauce so heavily.

Dick Francis takes a few months to complete his research, a few months at the keyboard to write his novel and spends the rest of the year traveling and/or promoting his books, which appear annually like clockwork.

John D. MacDonald wrote from four to eight hours a day, six days a week. Mickey Spillane, on the other hand, at least during his early years, would sit down at the typewriter, slip the end of a roll of butcher paper under the platen and keep typing for as long as it took to complete a novel. Then he'd ignore the literary process for a while, until his publisher called.

The first thing to realize is that your life-style and/or livelihood will always dictate your work habits and it would be a mistake to try to adopt the schedule of a novelist just because you like his or her books.

Due to changing employment circumstances, I, myself, have shifted into several different work patterns during my twenty-six years as a writer. My first, which lasted six years, was built around a nine-to-five job at a magazine. That leaves you few options. At least three nights a week, as soon as my cohorts would wander off to sample the happy-hour wares of nearby saloons, I'd clear my desk of the cares of the day and shift into gear on my own work, which then consisted of interviews, articles and critiques. I'd stay with it until the need for food or sleep forced me to call a halt.

That sort of moonlighting may sound grueling, but it was a walk in the park compared to my next schedule, which I adopted when I became a 100 percent freelance writer. What I had not realized was the importance of having an official end to the workday, after which I would be ethically free to pursue my private muse. Once I made the commitment to a freelance career, I never again felt that freedom. If I wasn't trying to meet a deadline, I was hustling new work. That narrowed down my time for creative writing to odd, very late nights and occasional weekends.

Under that system, it took me nearly three years to write my first novel, *Sleeping Dog*. And at least a third of that was completed during a period of two months when I steadfastly refused to do any major journalism projects. Fortunately, the success of that book allowed me to alter the emphasis of my schedule. Since 1986, I have been fitting my nonfiction work around my book writing, being much, much choosier about accepting magazine and newspaper assignments.

But I'm still forced to push my current manuscript aside from time to time. I write four monthly columns — on theater, film, audiocassettes and true crime — that take up an average of a day and a half a week. And then there are the odd movie and TV jobs that are hard to turn down because the money is so enticing. They're always we-need-it-right-away situations that force you to put the book on hold.

So, while I have long ago established a daily system of at least six hours a day at the word processor, I still haven't quite worked out which of those hours will be spent on behalf of a book or any number of other writing projects. How, then, can I help you with your scheduling problems? Well, unless your work history is identical to mine — and I wouldn't wish that on you — you shouldn't have a scheduling problem. You'll have a pretty good idea of the hours you can carve out of each week for your project. *The important thing is for you to make those hours count.* And there's where I *can* help you by describing some of the techniques I use.

1. I welcome the occasional insomnia. Usually, I can nod off without much effort, sometimes in a roomful of nattering people. But on those nights when sleep won't come, I'm not unhappy. I never try to force it. Nor do I get out of bed to read or watch TV. What I do is think about the book in progress, going over the construction of the chapter I'll be working on as soon as I get a chance. Either of two things happens: the mental effort puts me to sleep, or I wind up with a totally thought-out chapter.

2. I try to use the novel (or short story) to push personal problems out of my mind. Easier said than done, of course, but unless this is accomplished, you might as well forget about your book and spend the day going to the movies.

3. I let my dog walk me. Every morning, the earlier the better, I spend nearly an hour thinking about the book while walking around my neighborhood connected to my dog by a leather lead. My dog, a Bouvier built like a bear, seems to realize that I am not giving him full attention and usually he behaves himself. It is only on rare occasions that he feels compelled to drag me down an alley to get my attention. Here, the idea is to use every spare task — particularly those that require little or no thought — to prepare yourself for the magic moment when you'll get the chance to put words on paper.

For example, don't turn on the radio while you're getting dressed. Think about the book instead.

4. If there are any errands — from posting mail to banking to visiting the doctor — I get them done before starting to write. I don't know anyone who can make progress in short sprints of writing interrupted by forays into the real world.

5. Research — at libraries or other locations — should be completed before you start to write. When I'm writing fiction, I keep research to a minimum. It's too easy to get so overwhelmed by background material that your sorting and editing brain cells short out. You can't shake free of the volume of notes to write. The late Tommy Thompson used to refer to this destructive postpone-the-novel process as "the tar baby syndrome."

6. Before starting to work, I sort my mail, but I try to ignore most of it. The bills get put aside, unopened, until I'm ready to pay them. Likewise the flyers and promotional material. Magazines get thrown onto a pile that eventually tumbles over when it reaches knee height. I do read personal mail. (It goes without saying that checks and letters from agent and editor move to the top of the stack.)

7. Though the temptation is great, I don't screw around with my word processor. I've talked to writers who use the machine to communicate with other writers or play Championship Poker. I know enough about my computer to use it as a sophisticated typewriter. I have to force myself to put off fiddling with word counts or spell-checkers until I've decided to call it a day.

8. I rely heavily on my phone answering machine. If the writing is going particularly well, I'll even turn down the sound on the monitor.

9. When I turn on the word processor, I usually know exactly where I'm going with the story. I spend a short time reading whatever I've written the day before, making small changes. Then I segue into the new work. I rarely go back any further in the book than the previous day's work. What you want to do is finish the first draft before going back to check those opening chapters. Otherwise, you rarely get past the opening chapters.

10. I do whatever I can, short of losing friends for life, to avoid lunch plans. You may think you deserve a break, but you'll lose all the morning's momentum. Better to pick up a salad or pizza (to use both ends of the calorie scale) on your way to work.

11. I'm flexible about my quitting hour. When I was single, I'd often work until two or three in the morning. Now, I usually click off the computer at about six-thirty. I try not to quit at the end of a chapter. It's easier to start up again if you're in the middle of something.

12. Finally, there are times when, as a crime novelist, you'll be asked to participate in projects that aid and abet the mystery genre, like this handbook. Such requests will invariably take their toll on your work schedule and you should always turn them down. Just like I do.

CHAPTER 4

WHEN TWO HEADS ARE BETTER THAN ONE

WARREN MURPHY AND MOLLY COCHRAN

There are lots of reasons why writers collaborate on novels:

- Differing areas of expertise.
- Time schedules that don't permit round-the-clock attention to one project.
- Mutual support.
- And the simple fact that misery loves company.

If the collaboration works, it's wonderful. But if it doesn't, it can make *The War of the Roses* look like a day in the life of Ozzie and Harriet.

A writing collaboration is, in fact, much like a marriage. We should know since we have both. And the question we're asked most often — after the obligatory *Where do you get your ideas?* — is *How do you work together?*

Well, there's a short answer and a long answer. The short answer is: the same way we live together . . . by agreeing and disagreeing, in harmony and chaos, in good times and bad, till death do us part.

The long answer is more complicated. In fact, there are two long answers since there are two of us. So here goes.

Question. *How do you begin a novel?*

Cochran. Every writing team is different because people have different personalities. Warren and I happen to be talkers — world-class, earsplitting, oral expulsive, marathon chatterboxes to whom no thought is real until it is repeatedly voiced. So naturally our novels start with our conversations. We push an idea back and forth like a snowball until it's big enough to become a novel.

Then I keep talking about the book and Warren tunes out, having immediately lost interest in any details of plot, preferring instead to discuss more pressing matters such as how the shape of one's nostrils determines one's sexual preference.

So the conversation continues, with each of us talking about a different subject. This is a confusing time in the creative process since, without constant vigilance on my part, the novel's protagonist is likely to develop odd-shaped nostrils. Eventually, though, I know enough about the story to begin an outline. When it's finished, twenty or thirty pages later, we start talking again.

And then I write the book.

Murphy. Oh? And what do I do? Lie around sucking bonbons? Anyway, the important point here is that we begin a collaborative novel with an outline. I think an outline will improve the work of most solo novelists, but in the case of collaboration, it's absolutely essential so you don't have two people writing off in all directions at once.

Question. *Do you work together physically, in the same room?*

Cochran. No. We have separate offices and rarely see one another at work. Before we were married, we rented a work space together briefly and the only thoughts that came into my mind were homicidal. Warren likes to watch TV game shows while he writes. He shouts out the answers to the questions while typing furiously. Then every hour on the hour, he turns on the radio — while the TV game shows are still going full volume — to hear the stock market reports. I believe this era in our collaboration ended at knife point.

Murphy. That shows how little she knows. I packed away the TV and stopped watching game shows years ago when I found out that Bob Barker was a liberal. And I know writers who *do* collaborate in the same room and it seems to work for them. Do you detect the existence of a bottom line here? Whatever works . . . and that's a function of the personalities of the two writers involved.

Question. *But isn't it important to know what your partner is doing?*

Cochran. Not very. While I'm working on the first draft of our joint books, Warren is doing something completely different and we don't really discuss our work with each other while we're in the middle of things. This is the period when we devote our entire attention, as a team, to the shape of people's nostrils. But every team has to find its own way and each works differently. We know two collaborators who write consecutive chapters of the same book at the same time, then sit around in the evening, reading to each other and criticizing each other's work. That makes me shudder but it works for them.

Murphy. Faith is important. The only time I'd worry about what my partner was doing was if he or she wasn't writing but was mincing around, *angsting* it up all over the place. Short of that, I'm not interested in work in progress because if I get WIP, then I've got to talk about it and I don't like to talk about writing until it's all done.

I've been lucky to have two terrific partners, Molly and the late Dick Sapir, and each of those partnerships worked differently. With Molly, she does the first draft of the book and gives it to me to fix (and then sits on the floor outside my office door listening for the scratching of my pencil on her perfect prose). Dick and I did fifty books together totally differently. Dick wrote the first half, shipped it to me, and then didn't care how I finished the book. Both ways worked, so I guess it's not really important to know what your partner's doing, just so long as he is doing *something.*

Question. *Whose idea is it that becomes the novel?*

Cochran. What difference does it make?

Which is to say, usually they're Warren's ideas. But he's still got crummy toenails. He snores, too.

Murphy. Ideas — gimmicks or McGuffins, if you will — are a dime a dozen.

If you can read page six of the New York *Post* for a week and not come up with a half-dozen book ideas, you're not cut out for this work. You just sort through them until you find one that both partners think is interesting and then that's the one you use. After that comes the hard work of making that idea into a well-plotted story that will carry a book.

Question. *What happens when you disagree about your work?*

Cochran. We don't have many rules but we do have one for that. Our policy is that whoever feels the most strongly about a point in dispute gets the last word. It's not a flawless rule; sometimes one of us gets a wild hair about something and goes all passionate about it and it turns out to be the wrong thing. But nobody's perfect. A writer working alone would make that mistake a lot more often.

Murphy. We can translate that to Molly always getting her stubborn way. This is a good thing because it means I can blame bad reviews on her poor judgment.

Question. *But isn't one of you the "ultimate boss"?*

Cochran. They don't call my partner "Hitler" for nothing. But honestly, I don't think either is a "boss" when it comes to our work. The work itself is the dictator and both egos have to be subservient to what's best for the book. Otherwise, it wouldn't work. That's really what's at the core of a good collaboration: The book has to come first.

Murphy. Okay, scratch "boss" as an inoperative word. But somebody's got to have the ability to make final decisions, without protracted negotiations over each point, so that the book finally gets done. That normally will be the last person to touch the manuscript and in my partnerships, that's usually me because I'm the best typist and I get to do all the scut work.

Question. *Do you have to be friends to write together?*

Cochran. Since I've never written with anyone else, I pass. Although I don't think I'd want to work with someone I don't like.

Murphy. As they used to say in the Bronx, "So it shouldn't hoit." But friendship's not really necessary: Look at Gilbert and Sullivan. They couldn't stand each other and yet for years they turned out this ping-pong music that is deeply loved by Anglophiles and other musical illiterates.

Suppose you deal with a partner only by mail and never have to see him? There, friendship is irrelevant and cooperation is really all that counts. On the other hand, if you're working in the same office with someone and are with him all the time, being friends might lower the nation's homicide rate.

Question. *Earlier you mentioned "different areas of expertise." Example, please?*

Cochran. No matter how good a researcher he is, any writer writes better about something he knows and loves. And with two of you, you've got twice the number of interests to draw from. Also it's easier to work in an area you're not very familiar with if you know your partner is an expert. I would never have attempted a novel about a chess player — *Grandmaster* — regardless of how tangential the chess scenes were, if my partner wasn't a top-notch player. And I don't think Warren would have consented to a book set in postwar Japan — *The Temple Dogs* — without me.

Murphy. Hear! Hear!

Question. *What's the difference between working with a partner and working with — or as — a ghostwriter?*

Cochran. I ghosted sixteen books for Warren and others, and I've always felt that ghosting is a good way for a young writer to get started. It's a guaranteed payday for one thing and the fee often exceeds whatever advance an unknown writer might make on a book that's under his own name . . . if it's even published. Ghosting makes it possible to work regularly at writing and the practice is invaluable since no one learns to write a novel in a classroom.

Also, it's very freeing psychologically. Since the book isn't going out under your name, you don't feel the pressure to produce perfection. I know a lot of young writers whose fear has crippled them from the beginning, before their talent was able to develop. As a result, they write slowly and without momentum and their work is timid and small in scope. Ghosting lets you experiment and take chances. There's no applause at the end except your knowledge that the quality of your work has improved.

A partnership on the other hand is a heavier responsibility. Your name will be on the cover for one thing and you owe your partner more than you owe someone who's paying you for a fast first draft. If the book stinks, you know you had a lot to do with the smell. I've always been proud of the novels I ghosted, but the Murphy/Cochran books are like my children. If one of them gets a bad review, I'm devastated. That never happened with ghost work.

Murphy. Small demurrer. Because it was easy for Molly, she thinks it's easy for inexperienced writers to get ghosting jobs, but it isn't. I agree with the rest of the answer. A collaboration is just that—a partnership between equal members. Ghostwriting is an employer/employee relationship and the employer is boss. If you can't take that, don't ghost.

Question. *How is your partnership set up? Do you have a contract?*

Cochran. We don't, but I don't think it's a bad idea. We do share the same agent though, and we both sign our contracts with publishers.

Murphy. I don't need a contract with Molly because, through tricking me into marriage, she already has riparian rights on my blood. And in twenty-five years of partnering with Dick Sapir, he and I had only a handshake, but Dick was my best friend and that was an exceptional circumstance. With anybody else, absolutely have a contract. Do it once, do it as specifically as you can, answer any possible thing that might ever come up, and then put it away and hope you never have to look at it again.

The sad fact is that people always wind up in court over things such as "Well, I thought you understood that's what I meant." A contract avoids that.

Also, should the unforeseen happen, a contract that includes a survivor's agreement can make sure that heirs and creditors and people who don't have any business in your business don't get involved in your business.

Question. *So, on balance, are you basically saying that two heads are better than one?*

Cochran. Sometimes.

Murphy. Only if one of them's not empty.

Question. *Would you do it again?*

Cochran. Yes. There are a lot of pluses, and the minuses are correctable.

Murphy. Only with someone I respect and admire as much as my wife. There's not a lot of that going around.

CHAPTER 5

EXPERTISE AND RESEARCH

FAYE KELLERMAN

JONATHAN KELLERMAN

How Much Is Necessary? How Much Is Too Much?

Is it necessary to be an expert to write from an expert's point of view?
Some contemporary crime and suspense novelists do just that:

- Robin Cook, a physician, writes about doctors, in peril, solving heinous crimes.

- Aaron Elkins, author of the Gideon Oliver series, shares a background in anthropology with his fictional protagonist.

- Andrew Greeley, a priest, creates mystery novels that center on the Catholic Church.

- John Katzenbach, a journalist, uses his professional background to create a reporter protagonist in his first novel, *In the Heat of the Summer*.

- Jonathan Kellerman, a child psychologist, pens the Dr. Alex Delaware series. The hero: a child therapist-cum-sleuth.

• Lia Matera and Scott Turow, attorneys, each produce novels that allow the reader entry into the clandestine corners of the legal system.

Varying styles, but each possesses an unquestionable sense of technical authenticity.

Such a tight match, however, is by no means necessary to produce a successful crime novel or any other work of fiction. Most crime writers have, in fact, assigned to their protagonists professions and roles with which they've had no direct experience. This *needs* to be so for the crime novel to survive, because, though cops and private eyes with a talent for fiction do exist—Joseph Wambaugh, Paul Bishop, William Caunitz, Dorothy Uhnak, Joe Gores and Gerald Petievich come to mind—they comprise a very small club, indeed. The same need for flexibility applies to gender: If possession of female (male) genitals were necessary to write from a woman's (man's) perspective, a vast number of notable literary works would never have been created.

The operative word is *fiction*. We novelists make things up. Ours is a Walter Mitty world and that's the fun of it. We convince ourselves that we can write from any point of view we damn well please, because we have inherited the cloak of (or at least a shred of) authorial majesty. We can be American and pen English novels. Ninety-eight-pound weaklings with literary alter egos of Schwartzeneggerian proportions. Our private eyes, mega-cops and super-spies engage in stunts that, in the "real" world, might very well result in revocation of license, criminal prosecution, or ignominious death. Our characters may be immune from basic physiological needs if eating, drinking, healing, etc. get in the way of telling the story. And though their creators may be inept at putting together a jigsaw puzzle, our sleuths are able to solve crimes of Rubik's Cube complexity with elegance and panache.

It's all part of The Great Mystery Fiction Geneva Agreement: We provide the thrill. The reader suspends disbelief, allowing members of the clergy, barkeeps, dentists, cabdrivers, college professors, senior citizens with no discernible source of income, and even animals, to get to the root of felonies and horrors that stump the law enforcement experts. In some cases, the insult to the gendarmie is carried to the point of injury: the expert is written as a mere foil—a straw person set up to be mulishly stupid so *our* guys can walk right over them.

A grand seduction, this crime fiction business, not wholly unlike a quick-shuffled Three-Card Mental Monte. But to pull off the scam, the *illusion* of authenticity is necessary: enough sense of place and time to get the mark to grab at the lure, but not so much technical information that he loses interest.

How then can knowledge and expertise, obtained either through direct experience or research, be optimally exploited?

There are no commandments etched in stone, but a few suggestions come to mind:

Technical data should never interfere with the flow of the story, nor should it be so jargon-laden or esoteric that only another "expert" understands what you're trying to say. Spare the reader lengthy recitations of statistics or verbatim transcripts of lectures you've received from your sources. And don't talk down to the reader. A sure sign of weak or amateurish writing is over-inclusion — trying too hard to explain too much, too quickly.

Transfer of information should sound natural, never pedantic. Unless, of course you're trying to create a pedantic character (a risky business, at best). The reader should never be yanked out of reverie of the story and say to herself, "Aha, this guy is trying to *teach* me something."

The data should be *interesting*. Some fields of endeavor are just inherently more interesting than others. But all fields are composed of both the interesting and the dull — usually a soupçon of the former struggling to maintain integrity while swimming in a vatful of the latter. Concentrate on the fascinating. The part that would turn *you* on if you read it in someone else's book. Resist the pressure to include everything you've just learned about the mating habits of the aboriginal yellow-footed tree frog just because it's taken you a month to learn it.

The expertise should be *germane* to your story, both in terms of plot construction and the development of character. Rewriting is especially useful in this regard. You may find yourself larding your manuscript with nuggets of esoterica that seem fascinating upon first reading but lose luster in the cold light of an editorial morning-after. Like a sculpture, the novel often takes form gradually. Don't be afraid to chip away until what remains is really important.

Here are a few examples of expertise-based prose that we feel work very well.

An explanation of voir dire from Scott Turow's *Presumed Innocent*:

> Late in the morning, questioning about the juror's backgrounds begins — this process is called voir dire, truth telling and it continues throughout the afternoon and into the second morning. Larren asks everything he can think of and the lawyers add more. Judge Lyttle will not allow questioning directed to the issues of the case, but the attorneys are

permitted to roam freely into personal details, limited largely only by their own reluctance to give offense. What TV shows do you watch, what newspapers do you read? Do you belong to any organizations? Do your children work outside the home? In your house, are you or your spouse in charge of the monthly bookkeeping? This is the subtle psychological game of figuring out who is predisposed to favor your side.

The definition of a borderline personality from Jonathan Kellerman's *Silent Partner*:

> . . . At first glance, they look normal, sometimes even supernormal, holding down high-pressured jobs and excelling. But they walk a constant tightrope between madness and sanity, unable to form relationships, incapable of achieving insight, never free from a deep, corroding sense of worthlessness and rage that spills over, inevitably, into self-destruction.
>
> Borderlines go from therapist to therapist, hoping to find a magic bullet for the crushing feelings of emptiness. They turn to chemical bullets, gobble tranquilizers and antidepressants, alcohol and cocaine. Embrace gurus and heaven-hucksters, any charismatic creep promising a quick fix of the pain. And they end up taking temporary vacations in psychiatric wards and prison cells, emerge looking good, raising everyone's hopes. Until the next letdown real or imagined, the next excursion into self-damage.
>
> What they don't do is change.

The printing of counterfeit money from Gerald Petievich's *To Live and Die in LA*:

> "Rick likes to do the whole printing all at once. He'll start in the morning by burning the images on the aluminum plates. When he finishes the plates, he puts the plate on the press and starts running off the fronts of the bills. Then he starts right off on the backs. . . ."

And Petievich on aging counterfeit bills. . . .

> "I buy me a plastic trash barrel and fill it with water. I

pour in a bottle of Creme de Menthe and about one bottle of black India ink. I soak the bills in the shit and then dry 'em with an electric fan. They come out perfect. The soaking and drying make the bills look dirty, like they've been in circulation for a while; takes away the crisp look that's a sure tipoff to the cashiers when you pass 'em."

Widely varying voices; but the common thread is the *simplicity* of the language. It may be useful to reread the above selections to appreciate this. All three authors are dealing with material well known to them because of personal expertise but generally unfamiliar to the reading public. Yet, in each case, not a single word has been used that would cause the lay reader to run to the dictionary.

Any time the reader has to sit back and analyze what you're talking about, you blew it. Unless, once again, the aim is to portray a character as being deliberately snobbish and confusing (e.g., a pompous blowhole using jargon to intimidate the opposition). This is not to say that specialized lingo is unacceptable. Like dialect, technical language can be utilized for verisimilitude and richness of texture. Just make sure that the reader can read between the lines of argot and understand what the character is saying.

Expert novelists often grant their greatest endowment of smarts to the hero of the story—following the old saw to write what they know, and/or luxuriating in the Walter Mitty ego trip that makes writing a better job than most. But don't underestimate the value of an expert *secondary character*. A couple of exmples:

• A forensic odontologist helps Detective Sergeant Peter Decker identify the charred remains of two teenagers in Faye Kellerman's *Sacred and Profane*.

• A pair of memorable entomologists at the Smithsonian Institute expose a vital clue by pinpointing the habitation of a rare moth—the trademark of a serial killer—in Thomas Harris's *Silence of the Lambs*.

So much for the use of expertise, once we've got it. But how do we get it?

The answer, of course, is research. And research is by no means limited to the uninitiated. Most fields of technical knowledge change rapidly and even the experts must work at keeping their knowledge current. What was standard procedure when a given source book was written may be outdated by the time the book is published. This applies to works of fiction as well. Sometimes, as in the case of Jonathan Kellerman's *The Butcher's Theater*, set in a city, Jerusalem, where events occur at breakneck pace, a specific date is used to anchor the novel in time.

The first step in researching, is obtaining the *flavor* of the field by immersing oneself in written material.

Articles in peer-review journals — technical periodicals whose contents are evaluated by experts prior to acceptance for publication — may be more current than books, but due to publication lag in academia, even they may be old news by the time they make it into print. Libraries — especially university facilities — are likely to include in their holdings newsletters and bulletins that offer maximal freshness. Scan a year or so of these to get a feel for what's been done. This may be less than a grand frolic: professional journals often possess all the excitement of a tractor manual. The literary mind screams: Where's the editing! But it's good to read the boring stuff, too. You'll know what not to do.

After you have a general familiarity with terms and concepts, the next step is find someone in the field. If you want to write from the point of view of a gynecologist, call up a gynecologist. Not every OB/GYN is going to chat with you, but you may find a few who are more than willing to give you some time. Some may even be thrilled. Especially if you give them an acknowledgment in your opus.

Many of us who've written cop or private eye novels have benefited from listening to what cops and/or PIs have to say. We've visited police stations, ridden in police cars, read crime charts and weapons manuals down to the individual firearm specifications.

All the information is out there. Footwork, a forthright manner, and a nice smile help reel it in.

As you amass your information, try to organize it in a way that suits your novel. Index cards or their computerized counterparts work wonders. Multigenerational and historical mysteries, especially, may require heroic feats of organization.

Live with the data until your confidence level rises. Try to think and feel like an expert. But don't fake it. If you don't know what you're talking about, leave the information out or ask an expert for clarification. Even if your facts are completely correct, there are detail junkies lurking out there, just waiting to pounce. It's much more fun to read their letters when they're dead wrong.

And speaking of fun, have some. If you love what you're learning, you're a lot more likely to transmit a sense of adventure and vitality to your readers. Fun's also terrific for its own sake: one of the most enjoyable aspects of professional writing is the opportunity to learn things we never had the time, or desire, to study in school. To sit in the stacks of a university library—just you and a bunch of musty old volumes no one else has touched in decades, to come upon the ultimate technical clue that helps your novel take final shape—is sheer heaven. Enjoy the luxury of exploring new worlds. Give yourself straight A's. There's no pop quiz tomorrow morning.

Chapter 6

Background, Location and Setting

Julie Smith

The backdrop of a mystery, the world in which the action takes place — the scenery, so to speak — has the potential to be as important as character or plot. Indeed, if painted vividly enough it can become a character in itself; or it can determine plot. It can set a mood, create an atmosphere. It can express an opinion. It needn't do any of that; it can simply add richness and color.

But it should do at least some of the above.

You could leave it out; you could set your mystery indoors and never give the reader any sense of the city in which the action occurs. But if you do, your work may lose a dimension. There are exceptions, of course — Stephen King did it in *Misery*, but we're talking here about the master of creating atmosphere; he aims for the claustrophobic terror of confinement and succeeds.

Failing such special effects, your setting must be rich and vivid and colorful if your mystery is to be first-rate. The reader should get a strong sense of it, a blast of grit and conflict if the story is set in Chicago, a cacophony of construction noise and yelling; the gentle feel and sound of lapping waves if the setting is Port Frederick, Massachusetts.

Describing the landscape will go a long way, but there are wicked, lovely ways of drawing out the power of a setting, making it release its essence, that go far beyond that. They are ancient ways in our genre, going clear back to Chandler's thirties. Consider the first paragraph of "Red Wind":

> There was a desert wind blowing that night. It was one of those hot dry Santa Anas that come down through the mountain passes and curl your hair and make your nerves jump and your skin itch. On nights like that every booze party ends in a fight. Meek little wives feel the edge of the carving knife and study their husbands' necks. Anything can happen. You can even get a full glass of beer at a cocktail lounge.

I'll never forget hearing Joseph Hansen, author of the Dave Brandstetter mysteries, lecture one cool summer night at a rustic lodge in the redwoods. "Put weather in!" he told his audience. And then, warming to his subject, he stamped his foot: "Put *weather* in!"

Yes, put weather in. But don't just say it's raining. Make us feel the sodden weight of a wall of water driven by winds gusting at sixty miles an hour. If a Santa Ana's blowing, make our hair curl and our nerves jump and our skin itch.

If the weather, the land, the milieu are to play an important part in your book, you may want to say so up front. Mickey Friedman's *Hurricane Season* begins with an artful prologue in which Friedman establishes her locale as an important character in her book, maybe *the* most important, but she is working two sides of the street here — her story takes place in 1952:

> Hurricane season comes when the year is exhausted. In the damp, choking heat of August and September, the days go on forever to no purpose. Hurricanes linger in the back of the mind as a threat and a promise. The threat is the threat of destruction. The promise is that something could happen, that the air could stir and become clammy, the heat could lift, the bay start to wallow like a huge hump-backed animal.
>
> If a hurricane came, there would be something to do

besides drink iced tea on the front porch and take long, sweat-soaked naps in the afternoon; there would be something to talk about besides how hot it is.

Palmetto is in northwest Florida on a corner of land that juts into the Gulf of Mexico. Tourists bound for Miami, or Palm Beach, or Fort Lauderdale do not see Palmetto or know about it. In their rush to the south, they do not pass near it. They want palm trees and hibiscus; Palmetto has scrub oak and miles of sawgrass through which salt streams meander, and acres of pine woods. It has broad, slow-moving brown rivers lined with cypress swamps.

Water is a presence, and people live in connection with it. They fish, or deal in oysters, scallops, and shrimp. On the beach road, there are fisheries built on pilings over the water, corrugated iron oyster shacks, shrimp boats, swathes of net. People travel by boat where the roads don't go — across the bay to St. Elmo's Island or down the sloughs deep into the river swamp.

Notice how Friedman first creates a mood — of stillness waiting to be broken. And then she uses geography to segue into rich description, along the way giving a painless, hidden lecture on the economy of the town. By the time we're on page two, we know what the place feels like, what it looks like, and how it makes its living. We're practically wiping away imaginary beads of sweat and we find ourselves on the way to the kitchen to make some iced tea. We now have a perfect picture of Palmetto, a veritable slide show.

In my own book, *New Orleans Mourning*, I used Mardi Gras as a vehicle for understanding the town. In an early chapter we learn, from the point of view of Skip Langdon, the cop, what Mardi Gras looks like:

The huddled masses stood several hundred deep on both sides of the avenue, some with ladders for their kids or themselves, some with toddlers on their shoulders, risking their kids' lives, in her opinion — one bump and baby hit the pavement . . . They really did holler and beg — just like the guidebooks said they did. It seemed to be proper etiquette for the hoi polloi. The aristocrats, (the male ones, anyway), grandly conveyed on floats, were supposed to demonstrate their largess by casting trinkets into the crowds. Little strings of beads, mostly, and Carnival doubloons.

It doesn't create much of a mood or even convey much information, but it does tell you what you'd see and hear on the street, a nuts-and-bolts item in even the shortest short story. This is the part of the tale where the fiction writer acts as reporter. She must be on the scene to record the sights and sounds of her setting, its tastes and smells too, if they're important. Then she reports; she takes you on a tour. I heard Joe Gores say once that he drives through the area he's going to write about, taking notes on a tape recorder, before he sits down to write.

But what if you have a scene in the Grand Canyon and you don't have a vacation coming up soon? Do the next best thing to going there — look at all the pictures you can find and interview everyone you know who's been there recently. But never cut corners by simply leaving out the description.

You can make it short; you can make it pithy; you can make it metaphorical and ambiguous. Just don't try to make the reader believe you're not mentioning what things look like because it doesn't matter — he'll see right through you.

Sometimes the feeling of a place is best conveyed by information other than description. In *Diamond in the Buff*, Susan Dunlap tells you more about Berkeley than talk of brown-shingled houses ever could:

> As I drove downhill I thought about Leila Sandoval and Berkeley syndrome . . .
>
> Like the street artists on the Avenue, Berkeley syndrome was a phenomenon that flourished here. Many Berkeleyans had come to town as students. Caught by political awareness, social concern, or artistic aspiration combined with disdain for material possessions, they had stayed. After graduating, or dropping out, they had worked for the good of their fellow man, or they'd followed their muse, sitting in the warm sunshine of commitment. They had stored good karma against the chill of a middle age they were sure would never find them. They worked twenty hours a week to pay the rent, but they knew they were not insurance or real estate agents; they were union organizers or metal sculptors. And, in Berkeley, everyone else knew that too. They were not ne'er-do-wells as they would have been back East, they were people "who'd gotten their priorities straight."
>
> Berkeley syndrome had blossomed in the Sixties, and bloomed well through the Seventies. By the mid-Eighties, the syndromees were well into their forties. Eyes that had

peered into blocks of stone and seen visions of beauty now needed bifocals; teeth that had chewed over the Peace and Freedom platform required gold crowns that part-time jobs would not pay for. And the penniless life with one change of jeans and a sleeping bag to unroll on some friend's floor was no longer viable. The need of a steady income became undeniable. And so they scraped together the money, took a course in acupressure, herbalism, or massage, and prepared to be responsible adults.

As it happens I live in Berkeley and can vouch for the fact that no citizen thereof will be able to read that passage without saying to herself, "That's my hometown."

Background determines plot when events are inextricably tied to the place where they happen. In my own *New Orleans Mourning*, I set the murder at Mardi Gras and have the motives and passions grow out of politics and societal attitudes that exist only in New Orleans.

Reaching back in history, Hammett's *Red Harvest* could only happen in the milieu where it's set — never mind that the town is imaginary, we'll never forget it. Los Angeles has traditionally been the American symbol of corruption, new money, recklessness, ambition, peculiar ways for society to go awry. Mystery writers have been mining it since Chandler, and now it seems as if a kind of Miami crime novel is springing up along the same lines.

Chandler's novels, for instance, could take place only in Los Angeles — they are *about* L.A. and its corruption. Ross McDonald's novels, also set in Southern California, could probably be moved to some other locale without losing much more than a few canyon fires and oil spills — they are *about* family secrets and the past affecting the present.

Tony Hillerman's novels have to happen where Navajos live, but they are about the Navajo religion rather than the land; yet the Navajo religion is deeply bound to the land. So the setting, though not quite a character in the Hillerman books, plays an integral part in their structure. A new author who lives in a unique locale, where events can be determined by the place itself, would do well to exploit it.

Background can also be used to express opinions, political or otherwise. An intimate acquaintance with the seamy underside of New York is a big part of what gives Andres Vachss's novels their bite and sting. Vachss uses the whole rotten social fabric as his scenery. When he zeros in on a street corner, you know just how his hero (and, one might imagine, the author himself) feels about it:

. . .Wall Street was expanding its way up from the tip of Manhattan, on a collision course with the loft-dwelling yuppies from SoHo. Every square inch of space was worth something to somebody and more to somebody else a few months later. The small factories were all being converted into co-ops. Even the river was disappearing as land-greed took builders farther and farther offshore; Battery Park City was spreading its branches into the void left when they tore down the overpass for the West Side Highway. Riverfront joints surrendered to nouvelle-cuisine bistros. The electronics stores that would sell you what you needed to build your own ham radio or tap your neighbor's phone gave way to sushi bars. Antique shops and storefront-sized art galleries shouldered in next to places that would sell you some vitamins or rent you a videotape.

People have always lived down here. The neighborhood used to be a goddamned art colony—it produces more pottery than the whole Navajo nation. The hippies and the artists thought the winos added just the right touch of realism to their lives. But the new occupants are the kind who get preorgasmic when you whisper "investment banking" and they didn't much care for local color. Locksmiths were riding the crest of a growth industry.

Vachss gives us social history and social comment all wrapped up in two neat paragraphs that also convey a pretty good idea of the look and feel of the place.

Notice how different a feeling you get from these two paragraphs and the description in *Hurricane Season*. Quite simply, you're transported—in one case to New York, in the other to Florida in the fifties.

And that, ultimately, whatever other functions it performs, is the goal of location and background—to scoop up the reader on a magic carpet and take him to the world of your book.

Seven Ways to Make Settings More Real

1. Don't treat background as secondary; use it to advantage. Set your book in a place that lends itself to atmosphere and exploit the locale to the fullest.

2. Use ordinary description, but go beyond it as well—give us feelings, sounds, tastes, smells, metaphors, impressions, opinions. As in all writing, show don't tell. Involve all five senses. Above all, give us strong images. Don't tell us it's a pretty day; show us the sun glinting through a violet canopy of jacarandas.

3. If it's appropriate, let the character of a place shine through and become a character in your book.

4. Don't cut corners. Visit the location of each scene, get the feel of it, take copious notes, then report. If you can't do that, research it well with books, pictures and interviews — especially interviews. Pay attention to people's personal takes on a place.

5. Don't overlook the obvious. If you're setting a cozy in Miami — probably a poor idea, but let's just say you've found an idyllic pocket in the suburbs and you want to plant a body there — at least *mention* drug smuggling; orient the reader to the larger community.

6. Note from the examples herein just how far a couple of paragraphs can go. Slip in nuggets of information — economics, history, social history, geography — but don't get carried away. A little does a lot.

7. Put weather in.

PART 2

THE PROCESS

CHAPTER 7

CHARACTERIZATION

REX BURNS

The importance of characterization is second only to an author's having something to say. In detective fiction, especially with a series, it takes on added importance because the reader must be convinced that the protagonist is capable of the physical or intellectual demands of capturing a challenging villain. Let me first discuss my selection of a central character and then go on to the topic of presenting characters convincingly. What I say here will be primarily for detective stories, but much of it can apply to other narrative fictions as well.

The old saw about imagining your character in full before you start telling the yarn may be a good one, but I've seldom followed it. For one thing, I have trouble knowing everything about myself let alone about someone else, fictional or real. For another, I don't have the patience to complete a detailed biography before I start a story's action. What I do find indispensable to start with is a sense, often vague, of the protagonist's personality. With Gabe Wager, the hard-nosed homicide cop who is the central figure in my series, I wanted a character with intense personal pride—at times to a fault—and the kind of leathery toughness designated by the Spanish word "duro." That was his nucleus.

The physical details followed—some more quickly than others—and were chosen to support this personality: a Spanish heritage (for the rigid pride) and short stature (for a bantam-rooster aggressiveness). He's also half-Chicano, half-Anglo. This was to heighten his isolation from both cultures and to emphasize the lone-wolf quality of his detection, a quality that so often puts him at odds with police bureaucracy. I'm not sure when I mixed his blood; it was before he had a name but after he had a soul, and somehow—given the soul—it seemed right that he be an "isolato." Gradually, but not until much later, I came to see him in much more physical detail: a small scar on his cheek, brown hair and eyes, sometimes a mustache. Usually, these characteristics would pop up as the story's development demanded. But the point is, these physical attributes (including his Spartan apartment and the Trans-Am he drives) are derived from his imagined core personality and from the requirements of the story's action rather than preceding them.

I followed the same process in creating Devlin Kirk, a central character I recently launched in a new series. But this time I was more aware of something I had only half perceived when I began with Gabe Wager: The personality must somehow be interesting. With Wager, that was an unexplored given; I was—and still am fascinated by the rigid personality surrounded by a fluid and at times chaotic world. But with Kirk, I actively searched my imagination for someone who could support a series of adventures and, one hopes, gather a following of readers. What would it take to provide such support? I'm embarrassed to admit how late in my writing career I discovered the simple answer: an intriguing personality. If the person interested me, I'd be more likely to hold the reader's attention.

Fundamental to this sustained interest is the question, "Will I be bored viewing the world through the protagonist's eyes?" If so, forget it; if not, go ahead and see what happens. The question has a lot of ramifications, entailing as it does the protagonist's quickness of eye, depth and agility of mind, and that ill-defined but vital thing called strength of character. Wager was primarily the result of a situation: What happens when a rigid figure tries to uphold the law in a world doing its best to be lawless. But that very rigidity narrowed considerably the spectrum of responses allowable. With Kirk, I purposefully chose a bright, well-read young man with a yearning for adventure and gave him just that quality. My hope, of course, is that throughout the series his mind will remain flexible so that I will not grow tired of seeing the world through his eyes. As with Wager, however, the nucleus of this protagonist wasn't physical appearance but a sense of his personality: quick-witted, self-confident and daring, but with a strong element of reflective thought about the ultimate meaning of what he meets.

There's certainly nothing wrong in starting out with an image of a character's physical appearance—the only "rule" I've ever found in writing is "Do whatever works." But a protagonist usually requires some complexity of personality to sustain a reader's interest. Even with a severely one-dimensional protagonist such as James Bond, we can see Ian Fleming and, later, John Gardner offering more and more facets to his character, facets that have little to do with the tumultuous action that is the series' mainstay.

Another, and to my mind lesser, means of attracting readers to a character might—in contrast to the above—be called external. It tends to make use of props of some kind. One detective might, for example, grow orchids and be a gourmet chef; another might be a suave connoisseur of labels and brands. Whatever the prop, it serves to make the reader care about something out of the ordinary in the person, something that makes him stand out against the rest of humanity and thereby gives a cachet of expertise that heightens the probability of solving baffling crimes. With a central figure, however, the prop is often only a temporary eye-catcher, and the real appeal is found in the character's personality.

The same external technique is often of help in quickly portraying villains and secondary figures. Think of the number of evildoers or sidekicks who are marked by an idiosyncratic quirk of behavior or a startling physical appearance. This verges on caricature, but there's no problem there; Dickens raised it to a high art, and a writer could do worse than to emulate his economy and clarity in presenting memorable figures. Indeed, in a story that's primarily adventure, there's often too little room for more than one "rounded" or complex character, and the yarn's rapid movement demands the economy of characters whose personalities can be summed up in a single phrase—"tough but kind," or "oily and cowardly." The trick, of course, is to present such characters so they don't come across as clichés. How this is done exactly, I'm not sure. I try to find a balance between such a figure's central motif and his probable human behavior in the novel's various situations. Perhaps with more time onstage, this kind of person could grow into complex roundness—the potential is there. And perhaps that's what I'm trying to say: A convincing "flat" character is one who has the clear potential of becoming "round," but is not given the opportunity in the flow of the story.

The use of props for external definition of a character is obviously a means of presenting character. But I don't think it's the primary one. To my mind, voice is character. By that I mean the narrative voice that tells the story as well as the dialogue spoken by the characters. If a story's in first-person point of view, this primacy of voice is self-evident; the reader is addressed directly by someone ("I") who saw the action and is telling about it in his own words.

Like the direct address to the reader, internal monologue or stream of consciousness can also serve to establish or advance our sense of who a character is. My Gabe Wager yarns are told in the restricted third-person point of view so that the reader knows only what Wager knows, and when occasion demands, the reader can also know what's going on in his skull. Here's an excerpt from a longer passage in *Ground Money*; it's intended to give not only a glimpse of Denver, but also of Wager's detached and even sarcastic assessment of his hometown, an attitude that tells us something about Wager's personality:

> . . . all over Denver Wager had seen a larger number of couples, many with children, setting up life in apartments and sharing houses with others. There was a touch of irony about that, for these were Anglos, the children of those who had taken their tax money out of the city to fill the surrounding suburbs with split-levels on lanes and drives and circles. Here their offspring were gradually developing the same kind of crowded and noisy neighborhoods Wager had grown up in. Now all they had to do was put in a corner grocery and a cantina and call it progress.

The clearest and often the most subtle means of presenting character is through dialogue between two or more speakers. In the following abbreviated passage from *Avenging Angel*, Wager and Axton are interviewing a man who discovered a body. I tried to let their voices reveal their states of mind as well as the orchestrated approach that Wager and Axton use on witnesses:

> "You guys believe me, don't you?"
> Wager looked at the witness. "Any reason we shouldn't?"
> "No! But . . . I mean . . . all the questions. . . . Honest to God, Officer, I was just hitching along here!"
> Axton nodded. "We understand that, Mr. Garfield. We just want to get everything down now so we don't have to call you up later."

Garfield sucked in a breath. "Yeah. It's just all of a sudden I thought, Jesus, what if you guys think I did it?"
"We don't know who did it," Wager said. "Yet."

A worried and nervous witness, phlegmatic Max, and an abrasive
and aggressive Gabe — these are the character traits I tried to let the dialogue reveal directly to the reader.

Note the lack of adverbs in the above swatch of dialogue. Wager
doesn't say "grimly"; Axton doesn't speak "kindly"; the witness doesn't
stutter "nervously." The diction and syntax of the dialogue, in conjunc-
tion with the situation of the speakers, will — I hope — carry the very sound
of the voices, so that the extra baggage of instructing the reader how to
read isn't necessary. In fact, it's a good exercise for writers to strike out
the adverbs and see if the dialogue can stand on its own. If it can't, then
in most cases I would guess the writer doesn't have a clear sense of the
voice — he doesn't hear the individual tones and word choices that make
every person's language his own. And that's simply another way of saying
he doesn't have a sense of his character.

In most fiction, character consistency is more effective than inconsistency, because the reader becomes oriented to a specific voice and
behavior that have been given a name. But character consistency doesn't
mean a lack of character change. For a long time, short fiction, especially,
was built around the moment of character change; and many of the longer
forms still trace a personality's journey from one condition to another.
The so-called rounded characters are almost forced to undergo some kind
of change because they're sensitive people who have faced some traumatic
action. This is especially true in a series in which each volume is like a
long chapter of an extended work. But the change in character generally
should be consistent in order to be believable. This is another way of
saying that, for me, character change comes from within and is based
on the established personality. Sometimes, abrupt character change is
explained as the result of an outside agent such as a demonic possession
or chemical imbalance from a faulty experiment. But even in gothic fiction
or sci-fi, the reader is offered some explanation to make that change
plausible within the world of the novel ("experimental" fiction is a different game with different rules). In realistic fiction, such outside agents of
radical change are generally unconvincing unless they're couched in terms
recognizable in the real world which that fiction mirrors — head trauma,
dope addiction, degenerative disease, etc.

Most often, a character's change is more slowly paced and has a
quality of inevitability about it. I've found that once a character is clearly

established in the mind, then the probability of that character's actions can be projected. The result is the kind of change and the development I'm talking about. This is also the root cause of that delightful surprise when characters "take over" and the author seems to become less a creator than a reporter of what the characters tell him.

The characters in fiction come from the world around us and from within. What is it we're interested in about ourselves? What is it about neighbors and acquaintances that attracts us? What's the most fascinating personality we've met? Who would we like to be? What evil or despicable aspect of our lives or the lives of others intrigues us? Out of these and other questions come the nucleus of character and the character's own voice. But just as our lives are modulated by the restrictions of social behavior, so the lives of fictional characters are modulated by the demands of fictional structures. The characters in novels who loom in my mind are those who somehow find the right balance between the thrusting, vital energy of their lives and their roles as contributing figures in a narrative tapestry.

CHAPTER 8

WRITING A SERIES CHARACTER

SARA PARETSKY

> Amy [graciously] criticised the artistic parts of the story,
> and offered hints for a sequel, which unfortunately couldn't
> be carried out, as the hero and the heroine were dead.
> — *Little Women*

The death of the hero need not spell the demise of a series character, as Conan Doyle found to his dismay. In general, though, a story that brings decisive closure to the protagonist's life precludes a series about that character. Closure need not entail the death Jo March meted out for her heroes. Instead it means the decisive resolution of conflicts plaguing the protagonist in such a way that a sequel can destroy or intrude on the reader's relief in the resolution. In a story suited for a series, the resolution of plot conflicts becomes more important than that of character conflicts, however credible and intriguing the central character may be.

Peter Dickinson, one of the greatest of contemporary crime writers, has done both series and non-series work. His Inspector Pibble books all deal to some extent with the problems of a man who is an outsider, by temperament and upbringing, both to the police force, and to the world of financiers or landowners whose crimes he is supposed to solve. His intelligence and perceptions are such that he can figure out who committed the crimes without much difficulty. But to impose a solution on a society that regards him as alien remains a major hurdle for him.

Over the course of the series, Pibble nags at this problem from different angles. It is only in the final — or at least most recent — book *One Foot in the Grave* that he is truly triumphant. And to triumph he has to become extremely disconnected from normal life: Dickinson gives us an indigent, elderly, infirm Pibble stuck in a dreadful nursing home. He is not there undercover — he is there as one of society's discards. But he finally masters both his physical incapacity and his anomie. With *One Foot in the Grave* Dickinson has resolved the central problem of his character, and the series feels complete.

In contrast is Dickinson's *King and Joker*, one of the most brilliant crime novels of the last decade. The book tells the story of the coming-of-age of a royal princess in Buckingham Palace. The two main characters are a thirteen-year-old girl and her ninety-plus nurse, disabled by a stroke and dying. Dickinson's poignant, empathic presentation of these women — one just starting her life, the other ending it — is awe inspiring. The lesser characters are drawn just as credibly, and with equal care. At the end of the book, the major interest of the reader is not the solution to the crimes plaguing the Palace. It is Princess Louise's acceptance of her heritage, and the final tying of the knot in Nurse Durdon's life that enables her to die at peace.

These characters are so vivid, so beguiling, that Dickinson could not resist the temptation to bring them back in a sequel, *Skeleton-in-Waiting*. And in this book Princess Louise becomes flatter, less interesting. Her important problems were resolved in *King and Joker*. No one, even such a master as Dickinson, can write effectively about people whose major life issues have already found some kind of resolution.

If you have an idea for a story, or a character, or a group of characters, and you wonder whether you should be planning a series or a stand-alone book, you should think the matter through along the lines of the Dickinson stories. The first question you have to ask is what kind of story you want to tell. In particular, you need to think about what kind of problem you want to solve.

The last thing that should influence you is what you think publishers want, or what you think may sell. Writing to a hypothetical, unknowable marketplace instead of from your interests is the best way to produce flat, uninteresting work. A decade ago many publishers thought the private eye story was dead and didn't want to see such manuscripts. But people in love with the form continued to write in it. And because they wrote what interested them they created stories that have found a receptive readership.

Some publishers are now saying that the tough, independent woman investigator is passé, and that books of the nineties will hark back to softer women such as Mrs. North, working in tandem — perhaps even in subordination — to clever, strong men. Even if I believed such prophecy, for me to abandon my tough, independent investigator for that mythical market would mean I was writing something I didn't believe in. And if I can't believe in it it's a cinch no reader will.

Almost any form of the crime novel is suitable for a series: Amanda Cross and Emma Latham have created long-running, successful books with professional people turned amateur sleuth; George Smiley makes his weary way through Le Carre's spy stories; and police officers and private eyes almost demand a series. It's not the type of book you want to write that determines whether or not you have a character suited for many stories, but how you see the story itself.

All my own books so far have been first-person private eye novels with the same protagonist, V.I. Warshawski. Although I see her as a fully realized character, I also see her in relationship to a variety of stories. At this point I'm interested in such social questions as how large institutions affect the lives of ordinary people, and how the criminal justice system treats large-scale white-collar crime. These are issues for which I don't have a personal answer, and so I keep exploring them. They seem to be best addressed through the voice of my series character, rather than in stand-alone thrillers.

My detective has certain conflicts in her life for which I also don't have answers. These lie primarily in a tension between her need to be alone and her need for intimacy. The story that resolved that conflict for my hero would probably be the last in the series, just as *One Foot in the Grave* becomes the final Pibble story by resolving Pibble's personal issues.

In addition, solving my detective's personal emotional problems would mean telling a much different kind of story than the ones I've written so far. In series books, the emphasis is on solving the crime: finishing the plot. If the focus became the detective's conflicts, with the plot problems secondary, then I'd be better off with a stand-alone book such as *King and Joker*.

If you think your story idea, or your character idea, will work best with a series character, you should consider some of the special advantages and pitfalls of using a recurring hero.

The major problem with a series character is the need for continuity, but a continuity with enough change that the reader sees you are not going through rote motions in succeeding books. You have to show your hero — perhaps fat, a gourmet, an orchid fancier — in such a way that the reader who has read all your books learns something new, while the reader who's seeing your hero for the first time can understand him pretty completely.

This is a relatively small technical problem, and can be fixed by extending the hero's skills, as Sayers does with Lord Peter Wimsey, or presenting him from the viewpoint of a different character.

In *Strong Poison* we learn about Wimsey's virtuosity with music through the eyes of Miss Murgatroyd, for whom he plays a Bach sonata "with a curious impression of controlled power, which, in a man so slight and so fantastical in manner, was unexpected and even a little disquieting." In *Murder Must Advertise* she makes his grace and athletic prowess apparent in the scene where he dives from the top of a fountain into a shallow pool, and again when she presents his skill as a cricketer. These are all ways in which a highly skilled writer shows, rather than describes her hero.

When you are writing your first book, and the first of many books about your hero, you want to avoid annoying characteristics that may come back to grate on you in future books. Harriet Vane, the crime-writer heroine of the Sayers series, wishes that she hadn't made her own detective, Robert Templeton, a man with a taste in violent checks and plaids.

People with whom the hero associates regularly — family, colleagues, police friends or adversaries — have to be portrayed consistently from book to book. Arthur Maling has been heard to moan over his Potter series, because in the first book he gave the man partners and gave all the partners families. These characters have to be moved consistently from book to book. It's considered cheating to kill them off.

You should keep some kind of file on the salient traits and facts of your recurring characters. One of my own people is a doctor with a storefront clinic. Because I thought I remembered important data I didn't find out until after my fourth book was published that I'd moved her clinic by more than a mile. It's too late to fix that blunder now.

One of the most serious issues to decide is how to let your character change. Will she/he age? At the rate of a year per decade, or not at all, or with the passage of time as it affects you, the writer? Christie let Poirot and Miss Marple age very slowly, but she felt she had made a mistake in starting two series with heroes whose ages were already well advanced.

Sayers supposedly thought that Wimsey was too much a buffoon in her earliest books and tried to invest him with seriousness, and a love life in the later ones. Some readers find the last few books heavy and clumsy compared to the early ones. Sayers changed her hero but not necessarily for the better. Whether it was a good alteration or not, she worked it out quite carefully. In the passage cited above from *Strong Poison* we get one of several cues the book provides on the deeper aspects of Wimsey's personality — of the controlled power his mask of buffoonery hides. *Strong Poison* provides all the clues to the change in Wimsey's affect that becomes fully realized in *Gaudy Night*.

Other detectives change without so much conscious direction from their creators. Chandler once said he thought he was writing parodies of himself in his last work. Marlowe changes — he goes from scoffing at those who know Proust to spouting Shakespeare as he takes on a denser, more literary character — but he doesn't age.

Other series characters, like Nero Wolfe, remain relatively static. Wolfe and Archie don't age. There is an illusion of perpetual youth about Archie, but he does in fact lose his brashness in the later books. He develops a palate and becomes finicky about his eating. His speech becomes less idiosyncratic and more like Wolfe's. These are changes of which Stout may have been unaware.

As you yourself change, the way you see your characters probably alters as well. You cannot force yourself into an unnatural stasis; nor can you expect to be able to do that with your character. It is of course better to direct alterations in your character consciously, as Sayers did. Unfortunately, as I have learned to my sorrow, that is much easier said than done.

A series character offers several advantages to the writer. The problem of change has as its obverse the pleasure in developing a set of people in detail, showing the progression of their lives, not abandoning them at one climax when we all know most lives have many pivot points.

The other advantage a series character offers is something I mentioned earlier in a different context: the opportunity to explore a set of issues from the same perspective.

In my own work, I didn't set out to create a series character. I was trying to prove to myself that I could write a novel. I wanted to write a crime novel with a woman protagonist. And because I live in the ultimate hard-boiled city, Chicago, it was impossible to think of my protagonist except as a hard-boiled detective.

As time has passed, though, the kinds of crimes that interest me, and the perspective that interests me, make the voice of my PI hero the most effective one to use. I find that she gives me the opportunity to look in depth, and over time, at issues of law, society and justice. I wouldn't be able to explore these as effectively in a stand-alone thriller. This does not mean a different writer couldn't do so, just that I can't do so.

For example, Dorothy Salisbury Davis's amazing novel *A Town of Masks* is a profound exploration of society and justice. She shows, with heart-wrenching poignancy, how the difference in our self-perception and the way our neighbors view us, can lead to tragedy. The characters in *A Town of Masks* speak with finality: There is no place for their lives to go at the conclusion of the novel.

Every crime novel can be written in a number of different ways. Every story I tell could be told as a police procedural, even as a spy novel, if you accepted corporate espionage as a form of spying. And most of them could be written as stand-alone thrillers. I choose to tell them as PI novels because I like that particular voice. It comes naturally to me. And I have a continuing curiosity about my character's life and those of some of her recurring friends and associates.

Chapter 9

The Amateur Sleuth

Nancy Pickard

Advantages and Disadvantages

In its simplest definition, an amateur in any field is someone who does not get paid for what she does.

She may be a "wannabe," that is, an amateur who is working for nothing, but only until the day that she begins to earn some money. Unpublished writers are that kind of amateur—which only goes to show that you can be very, very good at what you do, but if you don't earn a living at it, the world will still insist on calling you an amateur. In that sense, Vincent van Gogh—who never received a sou for his paintings—was an amateur.

Or, she may be an amateur in the sense of being a true volunteer—that is, she's doing the work for nothing, and she's doing it either because she loves it or because it furthers her ambitions or answers her needs that have little or nothing to do with money. That kind of amateur will never be a pro, because no matter how *pro*ficient she becomes, she'll never request or receive payment for her work.

The amateur sleuth belongs to that second category of amateur.

With that designation come all of the pitfalls of being a volunteer, whether it's a volunteer Candy Striper at a hospital or a volunteer crime solver. Those disadvantages are: first, you don't get paid. To borrow from the comedian, you don't get no respect. You get stuck with the dirty work nobody else wants to do. You feel a lot smarter than everybody seems to think you are. Not only do you not get paid, but you also don't get much gratitude, except maybe once a year at an "Appreciation Awards Banquet." The place wouldn't easily run without you, but nobody acknowledges that. If management would hire enough pros, pay them well enough, and if those pros did their jobs well enough, they wouldn't need you. You have to do it in your spare time. You have to buy your own silly uniforms. And, people are always patting you on your head (or worse) and telling you how cute you are, and why don't you run along now while the real professionals take over?

On the other hand, as a volunteer, you get a few perks that the real pros don't, to wit: You don't have to do it. You don't have to do it by the rules. You don't have to take it. You can talk back. You can quit. You can be late, or fail to show up, and they don't dare reprimand you, because they know they need you a lot more than you need them. And all that stands between you and retirement is your own conscience, which, however, volunteers seem to possess out of proportion to the rest of the populace.

If you decide to create an amateur sleuth to solve your fictional mysteries, those are some of the advantages and disadvantages that she'll face as she goes about solving the murders to which the professionals haven't a clue.

But what about you, the writer?

What advantages/disadvantages will *you* face in the creation of that sleuth?

The most important apparent *disadvantage* you'll face has to do with that familiar fictional term, suspension of disbelief. Which is to say, why is this amateur sleuth attempting to solve this murder? Why not let the cops do it? Why does this amateur sleuth keep tripping over dead bodies? And why doesn't she mind her own business? A private eye or a cop never has to face those questions, because solving the murder is literally their business.

For those of us who are lucky enough to write about amateur sleuths, it turns out, however, that suspension of disbelief is not actually much of a problem. Fans of amateur sleuth novels are *eager* to suspend their disbelief. They *want* to temporarily suspend their belief in the need for real police officers to investigate real crimes. They *want* to believe for a little while that a fairly ordinary, smart person (like themselves?), using common sense, sensitivity, good humor and fair play, can bring a villain to justice. For the time that it takes for them to read your book, they *want* to believe in the, perhaps, more idealistic, innocent and fair world that you have created; they *want* to suspend their belief in a real-life justice system that does not always work; and they *want* to suspend their belief in their real-life experience of witnessing unsatisfying endings to unsatisfying lives.

Your fans don't really want cops on the scene. If they wanted cops, they'd read a police procedural; if they wanted private investigators, they'd read novels starring those professionals. Your readers *like* amateur sleuths, so you don't have to fret very much about justifying the existence of yours.

Still, even though your readers love to watch an amateur solve the murder, and even though they may not want cops on the scene, in an amateur sleuth novel you will still need to make it appear at least marginally believable that the cops aren't any more than peripherally involved. There are many time-honored stratagems for getting around that obstacle. Sometimes the amateur takes over after the professionals give up on a case. Or maybe the amateur steps in because he or she has an intense personal interest in the case. Or it could be that the amateur is acting on the request of a friend or family member. Or maybe the amateur thinks the cops have botched the case — accidentally or purposely — and so she attempts to solve it herself. The amateur sleuth might even be romantically involved with a cop, and that brings him or her onto the scene. Or it might even be for the simple reason that the amateur sleuth happens onto the scene of the crime and follows the path of his or her natural curiosity about it.

I've used those stratagems — and combinations of them — in my Jenny Cain series. In *Generous Death*, Jenny gets involved in the case because her own life and livelihood, as well as the lives of some of her friends, are threatened. She has several excuses for getting involved in *Say No to Murder*: she is on the scene; she's romantically involved with the detective; and her own father is a suspect. *No Body* brings her onto the case at the specific request of her beloved former sixth-grade teacher Miss Lucille Grant. In *Marriage Is Murder*, she gets involved because she is so worried about the effect that the case is having on the detective she wants to marry. *Dead Crazy* sees her involved for three reasons: a "client" requests it; she happens onto the scenes of the murders; and she feels personally driven to solve the crime, because of family reasons. In *Bum Steer*, Jenny is a suspect, herself, always a compelling reason to find the real culprit!

A second apparent *disadvantage* that you'll encounter in writing an amateur sleuth novel is that most amateurs don't use weapons. Indeed, most of them aren't even trained in self-defense. By and large, they don't jog five miles a day, wear a Black Belt, or work out down at Gold's Gym three times a week. (Can you imagine Miss Marple lifting weights?) That means your sleuth will have to rely on her wits, and sometimes on whatever makeshift weapons she happens to have on hand, like knitting needles. Jenny Cain gets herself backed into a corner in her first adventure, *Generous Death*, and, in desperation, defends herself by attempting to strangle the villain with her (Jenny's) bra! In *No Body*, she uses her panty hose to tie up a murderer. Cops and private eyes rarely have to resort to such desperate maneuvers. Guns are quicker (than underwear). And remember: If you do teach your amateur sleuth karate, or train her at the firing range, you'll be edging her into the realm of the pros and away from the pleasure that readers take in watching an ordinary person make the best of an extraordinary situation.

A third apparent *disadvantage* to the amateur sleuth is that she needs some way to support herself that won't interfere with the plot. That's difficult to do if you give her a nine-to-five job. It accounts for why so many amateur sleuths are independently wealthy, like Lord Peter Wimsey and Mrs. Eugenia Potter. Lately, amateur sleuths seem to be attempting to live off more modest means: Claire Malloy and Annie Laurance are booksellers; Jane Jeffrey supports her three children on the modest income of her late husband's life insurance and his family's pharmacy. Other famous amateur sleuths are academicians with holidays, sabbaticals and summers off, like Professors James Owen Mega, Beth Austin, Harry Bishop, Kate Fansler, Peter Shandy and Gervase Fen, and schoolteacher Amanda Pepper. Or they might be actors, artists or writers—like Harriet Vane, Tessa Crichton, Jocelyn O'Roarke, and Patience McKenna—who are supposed to have at their disposal great chunks of free time. Or maybe they're medicos or clergy—like Sister Mary Helen, Rabbi David Small, Nurse Hilda Adams and Brother Cadfael—whose very professions make it natural for them to snoop.

When I created Jenny Cain, I decided to make her the director of a charitable foundation because I knew that foundations derive most of their funds from bequests. I figured that where there is money and death there is the potential for foul play. John Putnam Thatcher, the famous fictional sleuth who is the head of the trust department of a bank, enjoys many of the same detecting opportunities. Their jobs are basically nine to five and they do get paid, but that only makes them professional businesspeople, not professional crime stoppers.

The jobs of investigative reporter and lawyer would appear to be ideal for an amateur sleuth. But they're not really amateurs, since their actual job is to investigate the crime for their editor or client, respectively. Lawyer sleuths are admitted to the bar of the Private Eye Writers of America, so I guess we can't count them into the ranks of amateurs. Rebecca Schwartz, Willa Jansson and Howard Rickover are examples of fictional lawyers who have as much of the intimate, between-you-and-me charm of the amateur as they do the cool calculation of the pro. The same could be said of the fictional investigative reporter, Samantha Adams. But since those sleuths all get paid for investigating their cases, I guess we have to reluctantly draw the line at those professions, even though we'd like to include those characters in our club of civilized sleuths.

A *fourth* apparent *disadvantage* to writing an amateur sleuth novel is that you generally can't use as much bad language, violence, sex or gore as you could in some other types of mysteries.

And isn't *that* a relief? And isn't your mother grateful?

So it seems that even the apparent disadvantages of writing about an amateur sleuth can be turned into advantages.

There are other advantages to be had, as well:

For example, an amateur sleuth doesn't have to be an expert at anything, except perhaps at understanding people. As that archetype of the amateur sleuth, Miss Jane Marple, is often heard to comment, " . . . living all these years in St. Mary Mead does give one an insight into human nature."

The amateur sleuth also enjoys the advantage of great reader identification. We can all identify — assuming we want to — with an average Jane or Joe who just happens to stumble onto a crime and then just barely manages to solve it solely by dint of courage, wit and common sense.

In addition, the amateur doesn't have to be as "tough" as a cop or private eye, which has the advantage of opening the way for a more normal sort of character who is allowed to show more emotion than might be acceptable in a professional. Readers often say they feel as if they could sit down and have a cup of coffee with their favorite amateur sleuth. They might not feel quite so comfortable sharing a beer with some of the tough guys and loners who inhabit the darker worlds of private eyes and cops.

Another advantage to writing about an amateur sleuth is that you don't have to know nearly as much about police procedure (or guns!) as do the authors of private eye and police procedural novels. Sometimes you'll be able to avoid the police altogether in your novels; other times, you'll need to insert a modicum about procedure or weaponry, which you will verify by research—which can be as easy as calling a police department and asking.

There is one more apparent *disadvantage* to writing amateur sleuth novels. I've saved it for last because it is the one that you will hear most frequently and most passionately advanced by those few poor, benighted souls who don't care for the genre.

"Amateur sleuths," they object, "aren't real."

To which you may reply, "Pshaw."

Amateur sleuth novels don't purport to be about "real" crime fighters. What they *are* about is real feelings, real motives and the very real effect of murder upon people and relationships.

Like every other kind of mystery, including police procedurals and private eyes—in fact, like any kind of *fiction*—there is about the amateur sleuth novel a certain air of fantasy that its readers *really* enjoy. Maybe *real* life is not so civilized, maybe *real* murderers do not so frequently get their comeuppance and maybe *real* justice is not so commonly done, but mystery readers appear to have a *real* need to believe all of that is possible in this world. The amateur sleuth, like her private eye and police counterparts, allows us to believe in that better, more logical and reasonable world, at least for a little while.

It's a great advantage to you, the writer, to be able to provide that kind of pleasure for your readers.

CHAPTER 10

VIVID VILLAINS

SANDRA SCOPPETTONE

If the point of your story is "whodunit," the culprit needs to be worth the finding. Often the nature of the villain, and how absorbing a character he or she is, will affect the flavor of the whole rest of the story—as is certainly true of "Buffalo Bill" and "Red Dragon" in the novels (*The Silence of the Lambs; Red Dragon*) of Thomas Harris, to say nothing of Harris's riveting villain, Dr. Hannibal Lecter.

Often I start working out a story in terms of its villain. Sometimes he's more interesting than anyone else. I'm curious about what makes a murderer who he is. Was he born missing some human quality? Did his early environment shape him? Or was it a combination of both?

For a long time I was intrigued by "the nice quiet boy" who kills his whole family. When I decided to do a book about one of these kids, I first researched the subject. Had I made him a monster created by his family, there would have been no one to like, no one to root for. So I decided to give him a brain tumor. That turned into *Such Nice People*.

The villain in *Innocent Bystanders* was invented, but there had been a true crime case I knew of in which a patient murdered her psychiatrist's wife. Why? Was she in love with her doctor? Did she have delusions? What was her family like? Out of this came Hedy Sommerville and her family.

If you're going to go into the mind of a murderer, you should know something about his kind of pathology. All murderers are not alike. There are those who commit the so-called "crime of passion," the professionals (hit men, gangsters) and the sociopaths or psychopaths.

The reason I say *so-called* crime of passion is because I believe that this kind of killer is a narcissist. It is often a man who cannot bear rejection by his lover/wife, and rather than let her go on to a new man, a new life, he kills her. I don't believe that this has anything to do with love. Nevertheless, you can make this villain interesting.

To me, the least engrossing killer is the professional, who may be a sociopath, but does it for money.

What's the difference between a sociopath and a psychopath? Simply put, according to *The Random House Dictionary*, the sociopath is hostile to society, the psychopath is mentally ill. The psychopath usually kills victims known to him or, in his mind, is provoked to kill. The sociopath murders indiscriminately and often without any specific reason.

Charles Willeford creates this kind of killer in *Miami Blues*. He's Freddy "Junior" Frenger, and he's so fascinating that he almost takes the book away from Hoke Moseley, Willeford's series character.

The sociopath walks among us almost always undetected. In *Donato & Daughter* I created the character of Russ Lawrence. He's an upper-middle-class married man with two children. He's learned how to behave like the rest of the world and his family has no idea who he really is. I thought he was interesting in a horrifying way: writing about him was like watching an accident. Yet one editor said he was boring and wanted me to lose his point of view. I refused, lost the contract instead, but went on to sell the book elsewhere. And then readers wrote and told me how mesmerizing and chilling they found him. Sometimes we know better than editors.

The practical question here is how are we going to know how to write about the villains? Surely they aren't among our good friends or even acquaintances. So if you wish to understand their thinking, what do you do?

I read. I've read a number of books about the psychopath/sociopath. *The Murdering Mind* by David Abrahamsen, M.D. is an excellent book, giving insights into the perspective of these people. Others are: *The Mur-*

derers by Emanuel Tanay, M.D. with Lucy Freeman, and *Murderers Sane & Mad* by Miriam Allen Ford. There are many others that are valuable and that can be found at your library. One of the best is Tim O'Brian's *Buried Dreams: Inside the Mind of a Serial Killer*, which is written from the point of view of John Wayne Gacy, the serial killer from Illinois. O'Brian really gets into the mind of this murderer and the book helped me to understand the thinking process of a sociopath. Although Gacy wasn't an upper-middle-class member of society, he certainly was respected in his area and apparently fooled those who crossed his path, including Nancy Reagan.

Ted Bundy was a flawless example of the charming, good-looking sociopath who duped everyone. Almost any of the books about him are worth reading.

Another book that I used to research one of my villains is *Fatal Vision*, Joe McGinniss's account of Jeffrey MacDonald, who was convicted of killing his wife and two children. Again, MacDonald was the perfect portrait of a normal man: doctor, Green Beret, devoted husband, father. MacDonald denies his guilt. So what's new?

To my knowledge I've never had the opportunity to talk with a psychopath/sociopath but I suppose one could arrange this through a prison warden if so desired. From my reading I've learned that these killers are more than willing to talk about themselves, mostly to tell you that nothing is really their fault. In *Fatal Addiction*, an absorbing tape of Bundy's last interview before being put to death, he blames his actions on pornography. Right to the very end he eschews responsibility, as they all do.

I would love the opportunity to talk with one of these killers (in a safe situation, of course), but I suspect that I wouldn't discover much more than I have through reading about them.

Naturally, all villains do not fall in the above category. In most books, if the author isn't writing about a psychopath/sociopath, the villain's motive has to do with money or property. The jewel or art thief, the forger, the blackmailer, the bank robber are all such types. As well as the killer who knocks off his/her spouse/relative for an inheritance or insurance money.

In these novels, I believe, the plots are usually more interesting than the characters. Exceptions to this can be found in the books of Patricia Highsmith and Margaret Millar to name only two. Donald Westlake also creates engaging thieves.

One of the most well-known writers in the field, James Cain, created several books where the killers were seemingly ordinary people who, had they not met each other, (a *folie à deux*), might never have committed their crimes. At least the men might not have. In *The Postman Always Rings Twice* and *Double Indemnity* the main villain is the woman who seduces the poor besotted male into killing her husband, respectively, for love and financial gain.

In creating a villain of any type, motivation is essential. Even a sociopath can have a delusional motivation. In *Donato & Daughter* Russ Lawrence believes the murders he commits are totally justified. In *A Creative Kind of Killer* the motive is greed, and in *Razzamatazz* it's revenge. In the crime of passion, killing because he loves her so much (and it usually is a man) is, as I said earlier, a narcissistic motivation. Nevertheless, it is a reason, no matter how misguided and distorted.

So understanding your villain is essential. Although I never outline a book I do write biographies of my main characters. Even if I'm never going to go into the mind of my killer, before I begin writing the novel I know everything about him, from where he was born, to how he did in grade school, his hobbies, what he eats for breakfast, what newspapers he reads and even what deodorant he uses. Doing this, I also come to know his parents and siblings and his relationship to them. Writing this kind of biography can sometimes give you your motivation if you don't have one to start with.

I wouldn't be playing fair if I didn't say that sometimes my villains are based on real people, real cases. Newspapers and magazines are great sources for finding fascinating killers. I've spent hours in libraries looking at microfilm of old newspapers, searching for just the right killer. When I find him I make adaptations. Occasionally, I will even base his physical description on a friend. Once I was caught doing this and my friend wasn't too pleased!

To sum up, villains can be based on anyone. We must make our villains believable and not too sympathetic.

One caveat: whatever you do, don't make them more interesting than your protagonist. If you do, it will make your novel lopsided and might even sink it.

Chapter 11

In Search of a Novel

George C. Chesbro

Writing a novel is a long-distance run of the imagination and will, an arduous exercise, a quest, requiring stamina, discipline, confidence, patience, courage, technique and perhaps not a small amount of cunning in order to compete with that most problematic opponent of all, oneself. Writers need all the help they can get, wherever they can get it, especially when it comes to the critical preliminary phases of a novel when one is plotting the story line and planning the structure. It is folly to believe in, or profess, a single prescription for success in any phase of the essentially dark art that is the writing of fiction. Consequently, what follows is not a prescription, but a description of how this particular writer goes about the complex business of plotting and structuring; perhaps others will find the same approaches useful.

Plot is arguably the most essential ingredient in a mystery novel, which is the focus of our discussion here; a story must be told. Every story has a beginning, and the beginning of a mystery novel is an idea.

Therefore, the mystery novelist begins her or his quest by coming up with a single notion that can be squeezed, patted, poked, and fondled by the mind (a process I call noodling) to see if it might possibly yield up that spectral entity we call a plot — the conceptualization of a series of dramatic events that is the nourishment that must sustain the straining muscles of the imagination for weeks, months, sometimes years.

Writing is dreaming; anyone can dream, but not every dreamer can cause a dream to materialize by way of words on the printed page, strings of letters that may eventually entertain, enthrall, or even terrorize countless readers. A plot is simply a writer's dream that has been noodled, conjured up, from an idea. But where do these rich ideas that can cause altered states of consciousness in both writer and reader come from?

I have a boxful of them.

With very few exceptions, the plots for my short stories and novels have started out from a single item cut from some newspaper or magazine, or a scribbled note made while reading a book or watching some television documentary.

Somewhat of a news junkie, I read two newspapers daily, subscribe to a host of magazines and newsletters, and watch a great deal of television on PBS. Hardly a day goes by that I don't read or see something that pokes my curiosity and makes me think there just might be something there that could be noodled up into a novel. Over the years I've discovered that an initial idea can be more or less than it first appears; only time and wide-awake dreaming will tell. Since, as is often the case, I'm already at work on a novel when I come across such an item, I file it away for future reference.

Now, my filing system for notions is amazingly simple — a large cardboard box in my closet. This is my "boxful of ideas" into which I drop each day's collection of news clippings and notes, and it has been of inestimable value over the years in supplying material to stoke my imagination.

When I have finished a novel, recuperated, and am ready to begin another, I drag my boxful of ideas out of the closet, dump its contents on my office floor, and begin rummaging through this small mountain of paper. The only thing all of these pieces of paper have in common is the fact that at one time or another the information printed there caught my interest. Now it is time to noodle those notions, to see if any one or a combination of several, will yield a plot that will sustain me on the new quest I am beginning, the new novel I wish to write.

This dreaming, these flights of the imagination off the launch pad of a single idea, can, of course, be great fun. But an idea is not a novel, and at this point it should be stressed that creating a *plot* from an idea can be, and usually is, extremely stressful, difficult work. Authors who tell you about the book that "wrote itself" usually fail to mention the many hours, perhaps weeks, or even months, they spent *thinking about* the plot and planning the structure of the book that "wrote itself." While in the beginning noodling from a single notion may be entirely free, this thought process must eventually become more and more focused; the purpose of our flights of fancy is to finally catch *one* flight that will take us where we want to go: the land of the published author.

To help me focus my dreaming, I always keep "production notes," organized memos to myself concerning possible twists and turns a particular plot might take, names, titles (personally, I always find it useful to have a working title for my book in progress, since it gives me the feeling at a very early stage that I've at least accomplished *something*, but this is a personal quirk), casts of characters, locales, whatever.

In any case, write down everything that occurs to you, *as* it occurs to you; do *not* trust memory.

Eventually, if I am lucky, this increasingly focused *thought* process will lead to the *writing* process, the first step for me being a plot *outline*, a step-by-step description of how my story will unfold. I try to make this outline as detailed as possible, for I have learned that, for me, at least, the more effort I put into these preparatory phases, the fewer problems I will have in actually writing the book.

However, I have also learned that there is only so much planning I can do before I actually begin to write the book (by which I mean the first *draft* of the book; one should always bear in mind that rarely is anything of value merely written, it is *rewritten*, increasingly refined and polished through subsequent drafts). After all, we are talking about a *creative* act, which implies a certain amount of spontaneity, which by definition cannot be completely thought-out in advance. I will begin my first draft when my plot outline has become a kind of map, however rough, that will at least get me from one end of the land of my story to the other; I know the terrain at the beginning of my journey, the landscape at the end, and have some idea of the mountains I must cross, the rivers I must ford, in between.

Having done this, I am now in a position to receive one of the greatest thrills a fiction writer can experience: *discovery*. In the process of discovery, the writer begins the actual writing of a novel only to discover that all is not exactly as she or he had planned; the actual landscape of the novel is incredibly richer, more complex, than could have been imagined from the mere map, the plot outline, that has been made — this despite the many hours that have gone into drawing up that map! New characters appear, or characters you thought you understood suddenly acquire new personality traits. A path you thought would be easy turns out to be particularly treacherous, or vice versa. Of course, you continue to take production notes all through the writing of this first draft — a note to yourself that something will change at the beginning, plans for a different ending.

A dark art indeed! Let's examine how these processes I have described actually come into play in a specific example.

In the recently published *Second Horseman Out of Eden*, Mongo, my dwarf private investigator, and Garth, his big big brother, battle a very dangerous band of murderous religious fanatics for the body and soul of an abused child who has written a letter to Santa Claus to ask him for help.

I've always been fascinated by the inextinguishable propensity among human beings for superstition, and by fanatics of all flavors, and so I didn't need any further stimulation in that area. But the real genesis for that novel came while I was sorting through the contents of my boxful of ideas and came across a yellowed clipping (it had been stuck to the bottom of the box, perhaps for years). The article described how, each year at Christmastime, the main post office in New York City puts all the thousands of letters addressed to Santa Claus it has received in cardboard boxes, and places them on counters in the lobby for the public to browse through. Interested New Yorkers may take up to five letters each, the idea being that these people will express their holiday spirit and goodwill by responding to the requests in the letters, either by buying gifts and distributing them, or providing some service requested by the children who wrote the letters. In effect, these people celebrate Christmas in part by playing Santa Claus.

Fiction writers' dreams are made of such stuff, and novels noodled.

Mongo and Garth are New Yorkers, I said to myself, and, good men that they are, it wouldn't surprise me at all to find out that they are among the thousands of New Yorkers who select letters and play Santa each year at Christmas (I am constantly finding out new things about Mongo and Garth as I write about them, and am frequently surprised and delighted by the things I unearth about their characters in this long-range process of discovery). Now, what if one of the letters they select is from a little girl who is obviously being abused, and who is asking Santa to help bring her release from her pain and misery . . . ?

Another news item, this one from *Newsweek*, another idea to weave into the dreaming generated by the first. This clipping concerns a biological super-project, an attempt by an idealistic billionaire philanthropist to build totally self-contained environmental modules that might be used to house colonists on the moon, or even the other planets in the solar system.

What if our religious fanatics, who control the fate of the little girl in distress, are attempting to build such a structure, not to colonize the moon or other planets, but to be a refuge for themselves in the "final days," Armageddon, which they believe are upon us? Indeed, what if they have made plans to nudge Armageddon along by wiping out millions of people . . . ?

Noodle, noodle . . .

And what if the child, in her letter, says that she is being held captive in a "secret place"? What if there are traces of soil inside the envelope, dirt that only comes from the Amazon rain forest . . . ? And what if . . . ?

But you get the idea.

While news articles may provide a rich lode of ideas, they are not, of course, the only source. Overheard conversations, incidents in one's own life, a fleeting thought that seems to have come unbidden . . . Virtually *anything* can provide an idea that, with patience and hard work, may provide the genesis for a plot, the waking dream that becomes a novel.

After one has found a story to *tell*, the next problem that looms is one of structure, or how to actually *write* it. Specifically, who will be telling the story? One person, or several? From whose point of view does the reader view the action? This decision as to what voice to use can be crucial, especially in the mystery novel, since it may largely determine the sequence of action, what information is given to the reader, and what information can be legitimately withheld in order to create an air of mystery and suspense.

Perhaps the easiest way to tell a story is through the "eye in the sky," omniscient speaker, who is never named. This voice is not a character in the novel, but solely a narrator of events. Of course, the advantage to using an "eye in the sky" narrative is that the author may arbitrarily switch locale at any time, probe all of the characters' minds for their deepest secrets and darkest motivations, and provide any and all information at any time so as to keep the reader up to date on events.

Alas, the easiest way to tell a tale is not necessarily the best; the best way to tell any story, *particularly* in a mystery novel, is that which will generate the most suspense in the mind of the reader, compelling her or him to keep turning pages to see what will happen next.

For my novel, *Bone*, I employed a multiple-point-of-view technique, a structure in which the case is always third person, but the reader experiences events through the eyes, and in the mind, of one character at a time throughout any chapter, which can be of arbitrary length. This is the structure that seemed best suited to what was to be a psychological novel of suspense requiring the reader to know what was going on in the minds of a number of characters.

However, in all of my Mongo novels, I use the "classic" structure of the detective mystery, the first-person narrative. It is Mongo himself who is telling the story, and so the reader experiences events, thoughts and emotions *only* from Mongo's point of view, and discovers things only as he does. While the use of first-person narrative may be a more difficult literary device (if you want the reader to know what is going on in another locale, you must find a way of getting your narrator there, and, of course, it is impossible for the narrator to know *precisely* what is going on in anyone's mind but his or her own), I believe it particularly lends itself to the mystery novel.

The use of a first-person narrative structure requires considerable discipline on the part of the writer; the reader cannot simply be *told* things by the author, but must discover—or deduce—them along with the narrator. However, if the reader can be made to care about the narrator, and if the puzzle the narrator must solve is a good one, the reader will be compelled to follow along through the pages, since first-person narrative encourages close identification of reader and character, and this empathy, this sharing of peril in the reader's mind, is the key ingredient in the generation of suspense.

Yet another factor an author must consider in structuring a novel is the question of what *tense* the narrator will speak in. Most mystery novels are written in the past tense, with the narrator describing events that have supposedly already happened. However, some authors have successfully used the *present* tense, which tends to make the action seem more "immediate." In my two novels involving Veil Kendry, *Veil* and *Jungle of Steel and Stone*, I have employed *both*, using the present tense to indicate that this brain-damaged painter and "street detective" is dreaming.

There are no surefire recipes; indeed, there may be almost as many ways to plot and structure a mystery novel as there are mystery writers. The point is that attention *must be paid* to these two key ingredients if you hope to transport a reader into the world you have created for the few hours or days it will take to read your novel. A thoughtful disciplined approach to both plot and structure can make all the difference between a "good story" you might tell around a campfire, and a published book that people will pay to read.

CHAPTER 12

BUILDING WITHOUT BLUEPRINTS

TONY HILLERMAN

In thirty-seven years of writing, I have accumulated two bits of wisdom that may be worth passing along.

First, I no longer waste two months perfecting that first chapter before getting on with the book. No matter how carefully you have the project planned, first chapters tend to demand rewriting. Things happen. New ideas suggest themselves, new possibilities intrude. Slow to catch on, I collected a manila folder full of perfect, polished, exactly right, pear-shaped first chapters before I learned this lesson. Their only flaw is that they don't fit the book I finally wrote. The only book they will ever fit will be one titled *Perfect First Chapters*, which would be hard to sell. Thus Hillerman's First Law: *Never polish the first chapter until the last chapter is written.*

The second law takes longer to explain. When I defend it, I'm like the fellow with his right arm amputated arguing in favor of left-handed bowling. However, here it is: *Some people, sometimes, can write a mystery novel without an outline.* Or, put more honestly: If you lack the patience (or brains) to outline the plot, maybe you can grope your way through it anyway, and sometimes it's for the best.

I was in the third chapter of a book titled *Listening Woman* when this truth dawned. Here's how it happened:

I had tried to outline three previous mystery novels. Failing, and feeling guilt-ridden and inadequate, I finally finished each of them, by trying to outline a chapter or two ahead as I wrote. I had tried for weeks to blueprint this fourth book, sketching my way through about six chapters. At that point, things became impossibly hazy. So I decided to write the section I had blueprinted. Maybe then I could see my way through the rest of it.

I wrote the first chapter exactly as planned, an elaborate look at the villain outsmarting a team of FBI agents on a rainy night in Washington, D.C. I still feel that this chapter may the best 5,000 words I've ever written. By the time I had finished it, I had a much better feeling for this key character, and for the plot in which he was involved. Unfortunately, this allowed me to see that I was starting the book too early in the chronology of the story I was telling. So this great first chapter went into a manila folder (to be cannibalized later for flashback material). Then I planned a new opening. This one takes place now on the Navajo Reservation at the hogan of an elderly and ailing Navajo widower named Tso. It is mostly a dialogue between him and a shaman he has summoned to determine the cause of his illness. The chapter was intended to establish time, mood and the extreme isolation of the area of the Navajo Reservation where the novel takes place. It would give the reader a look at Tso, who will be the murder victim, and introduce the shaman, who would be a fairly important character. Finally, the dialogue would provide background information and — in its discussion of Navajo taboos violated by Tso — provide clues meaningless to the FBI, but significant to my Navajo Sherlock Holmes. Again, all went well, but as I wrote it I could sense a flaw.

It was dull. In fact, it was *awfully dull.*

I had planned to have the second chapter take place a month later. In the interim, Tso has been murdered offstage, and the killing is an old unsolved homicide. Why not, I wondered then, have the murder take place during the opening scene? Because then either (a) the shaman would see it, tell the cops, and my novel becomes a short story; or (b) the murderer would zap the shaman, too, messing up my plot. At this stage, a writer who specializes in Navajos and has accumulated a headful of Navajo information searches the memory banks for help. Navajos have a terribly high rate of glaucoma and resulting blindness. Why not a blind old woman shaman? Then how does she get to the isolated Tso hogan? Create a niece, an intern-shaman, who drives the old lady around. The niece gets killed, and now you have a double murder done while the blind woman is away at a quiet place having her trance. You also have an opportunity to close the chapter with a dandy little non-dull scene in which the blind woman, calling angrily for her newly deceased niece, taps her way with her cane across the scene of carnage. The outline is bent, but still recognizable.

Early in chapter two, another bend. The revised plan still calls for introducing my protagonist, Navajo Police Lt. Joe Leaphorn, and the villain. Joe stops Gruesome George for speeding, whereupon G.G. tries to run over Joe, roars away, abandons his car, and eludes pursuit. Two paragraphs into this chapter, it became apparent that Joe needed someone in the patrol car with him to convert the draggy internal monologue I was writing into snappy dialogue. So I invent a young sheep thief, handcuff him securely, and stick him in the front seat. He turns out to be wittier than I had expected, which distorts things a bit, but nothing serious goes wrong. Not yet. Leaphorn stops the speeder and is walking toward the speeder's car. As many writers do, I imagine myself into scenes — seeing, hearing, smelling everything I am describing.

What does Leaphorn see? His patrol car emergency light flashing red reflections off the speeder's windshield. Through the windshield, he sees the gold-rimmed glasses I'll use as a label for Gruesome George until we get him identified. What else? My imagination turns whimsical. Why not put in another pair of eyes? Might need another character later. Why not put them in an unorthodox place — peering out of the backseat of the sedan? But why would anyone be sitting in the back? Make it a dog. A huge dog. In a crate. So the dog goes in. I can always take him out.

Still we seem to have only a minor deflection from the unfinished, modified version of the partial outline. But a page or two later, in chapter three, it became obvious that this unplanned, unoutlined dog was going to be critically important. I could see how this ugly animal could give the villain a previous life and the sort of character I was planning to hang on him. More important, I could begin to see Dog (already evolved into a trained attack dog) could be used to build tension in the story. As I thought about the dog, I began to see how my unblueprinted sheep thief would become the way to solve another plot problem.

Since that third chapter of my fourth mystery novel, I have honestly faced the reality. For me, working up a detailed outline simply isn't a good idea. I should have learned that much earlier.

For example, in my first effort at mystery fiction, *The Blessing Way*,

I introduce the Gruesome George character in a trading post on the Reservation. He is buying groceries while my protagonist watches, slightly bored. I, too, am slightly bored. So is the reader. Something needs to be done to generate a bit of interest. I decide to insert a minor mystery. I have the fellow buy a hat, put his expensive silver concha hatband on it, and tell the storekeeper that someone had stolen the original hat. Why would someone steal a hat and leave behind an expensive silver hatband? My protagonist ponders this oddity and can't think of any reason. Neither can I. If I can't think of one later, out will come the hat purchase and in will go some other trick to jar the reader out of his nap. But the hat stayed in. My imagination worked on it in the context of both the Navajo culture and my plot requirements. It occurred to me that such a hat, stained with its wearer's sweat, would serve as the symbolic "scalp" required at a Navajo ceremonial (an Enemy Way) to cure witchcraft victims and to kill witches. When my policeman sees the stolen hat (identified by the missing hatband) in this ritual role, it leads him to the solution of his mystery. (And the author to the completion of his book.)

I have gradually learned that this sort of creative thinking happens for me only when I am at very close quarters with what I am writing—only when I am in the scene, in the mind of the viewpoint character, experiencing the chapter and sharing the thinking of the people in it. From the abstract distance of an outline, with the characters no more than names, nothing seems real to me. At this distance, the details that make a plot come to life always elude me.

Another example: In *Fly on the Wall*, the principal character is a political reporter. He has been lured into the dark and empty state capitol building in the wee hours on the promise that doors will be left unlocked to give him access to confidential tax files. He spots the trap and flees, pursued by two armed men. Before I began writing this section, I had no luck at all coming up with an idea of how I could allow him to escape without straining reader suspension of disbelief. Now, inside these spooky, echoing halls, I think as my frightened character would think, inspired by his terror. No place to hide in the empty hallways. Get out of them. Try a door. Locked, of course. All office doors would be locked. Almost all. How about the janitor's supply room which the night watchman uses as his office? That door is open. Hide there. (Don't forget to dispose of the watchman.) A moment of safety, but only a moment until the hunters think of this place. Here are the fuse boxes that keep the hall lights burning. Cut off the power. Darken the building. Meanwhile, the readers are wondering, what's happened to the night watchman? Where is he? That breathing you suddenly hear over the pounding of your own heart, not a yard away in the pitch blackness, is the watchman, knocked on the head and tied up. Check his holster. Empty, of course. So what do you do? The hunters know where the fuse boxes are. They are closing in. Feel around in the darkness for a weapon. And what do you feel on the shelves in a janitor's storeroom? All sorts of stuff, including a gallon jug of liquid detergent. You open the door and slip out into the dark hallway, running down the cold marble floor in your sock feet, hearing the shout of your pursuer, dribbling the detergent out of the jug behind you as you sprint down the stairs.

In an outline I would never have thought of the janitor's supply room, nor of the jug of liquid detergent. Yet the detergent makes the hero's escape plausible and is a credible way to eliminate one of the two pursuers as required by the plot. Even better, it is raw material for a deliciously hideous scene — hero running sock-footed down the marble stairway, liquid soap gushing out behind him from the jug. Bad guy in his leather-soled shoes sprinting after him. Except for describing the resulting noises, the writer can leave it to the reader's imagination.

A big plus for working without an outline, right? The big negative is that I forgot Hero had removed his shoes and had no way to recover them. The editor didn't notice it either, but countless readers did — upbraiding me for having the hero operating in his socks throughout the following chapter.

I have learned, slowly, that outlining a plot in advance is neither possible, nor useful, for me. I can get a novel written to my satisfaction only by using a much freer form and having faith that — given a few simple ingredients — my imagination will come up with the necessary answers.

Those ingredients — not in any order of importance:

• *A setting with which I am intimately familiar.* Although I have been nosing around the Navajo Reservation and its borderlands for more than thirty years, I still revisit the landscape I am using before I start a new book — and often revisit again while I am writing it. And then I work with a detailed, large-scale map beside my word processor.

• *A general idea of the nature of the mystery* that needs to be solved, and a good idea of the motive for the crime, or crimes.

• *A theme.* For example, *The Dark Wind* exposes my Navajo cop to a crime motivated by revenge — to which Navajos attach no value and find difficult to understand.

• *One or two important characters* in addition to the policeman/protagonist. However, even these characters tend to be foggy at first. In *Dance Hall of the Dead*, the young anthropology graduate student I had earmarked as the murderer turned out to be too much of a weakling for the job. Another fellow took on the role.

When I finish this, I will return to chapter eight of the present "work in progress." My policeman has just gone to the Farmington jail, where I had intended to have him interview a suspect. Instead he has met the suspect's attorney—a hard-nosed young woman who, as the dialogue progressed, outsmarted my cop at every turn. This woman did not exist in my nebulous plans for this book and has no role. But I have a very strong feeling that she will assume one and that it will be a better book because of her.

That's a good argument against outlines. Without one, I can hardly wait to see how this book will turn out.

Chapter 13

Outlining

Robert Campbell

For years, before the advent of the word processor, I never outlined my novels. Even when I was a screenwriter I resisted writing treatments. In both cases I preferred the method attributed to William Faulkner. When asked how he wrote his books he said something like, "I set my characters on the road and walk beside them, listening to what they have to say."

I've always strived for two sometimes seemingly contradictory qualities in my novels: the inevitability of the conclusion so that the reader, upon reflection, can see the shadow of the end suggested in the beginning; and the illusion that the writer and the reader are discovering the same things about the story and characters at the same time.

I try to include scenes or lines of dialogue or insights into character and motivation that will resonate throughout the book.

A man, when a child, has the courage to smash the life out of a fatally injured puppy suffering great pain. Years later, when he has the courage to assist a loved one out of the agony of a terminal illness, the reader will remember and understand. You as the writer will have made your case for the character's reasoning and philosophy in one place, saving the need for a too obvious explication in the later scene.

There's a great deal of difference for me in writing a book from an outline, which is, in a sense, the imposition of predestination on the characters and the plot, and embarking on a journey during which the book reveals itself or is discovered rather than being manufactured according to a blueprint.

This roving often leads to dead ends. To extricate myself, I am forced to retrace my steps to some fork in the road and set off on another path altogether.

But even such digressions prove valuable because I always get to learn a lot about my people along the path that didn't lead where I want them to go.

I think I might mention here that nothing is lost to the writer. Even discarded pages are useful, even if they've done nothing else but exercise the writing muscles.

Lately, I've come upon a technique that seems to offer the benefits of an outline and the freedom of the discovered way.

When I begin a novel I usually have a character or characters in mind. Not every one that will finally prove necessary to tell the story, but most of them. Not greatly detailed, for they are people just met who will reveal themselves to me as we get acquainted, but more than rough shapes.

Sometimes the initiating stimulus is a quote, a news article that engages my attention or a scene that for no reason I can usually understand has sprung to mind unbidden.

It used to be that I would simply begin to write, making a note now and then perhaps, pushing forward from front to back, wrestling the beast of form, listening sharply for the voice that would finally be the voice of the book, pausing, from time to time, in those terrible places where the writer wonders why in hell he or she had ever embarked on the project in the first place, the bones of the novel tottering, the language becoming as dry as dust, the whole effort turning into a disaster, yet somehow fighting on to the end of it, restoring order, polishing the words, refining the plot, getting it done as well as I was able.

Now I use the outline provision of my word processor to set up the document. If you haven't got such a facility, just make an outline as you used to do back in school or simply set down a line of numbers to represent the chapters you estimate the book will require.

I also create a number of documents. If your program has the capacity to create documents and stack them on the screen, it will prove invaluable. For those who handwrite or type draft material, these documents might be sections of a loose-leaf binder or separate file folders.

I create a Chronology, Cast of Characters, Address Book, Timeline of History, Notebook and a document I call Agenda, which sketches the goals, desires and probable actions of each principal character as I move along through the body of the book.

As a natural consequence of this last document the connections begin to form themselves, suggesting scenes and the flow of narrative.

Sometimes these documents can be placed between page breaks in separate sections at the bottom of the document that contains the novel.

If your program requires more than one document per book, simply move the information bits along from part to part as the book grows.

I tend to write chapters of ten pages, about 2,500 words, adjusting them for content, natural or dramatic breaks, tailoring them longer or shorter as I see the desirability of slowing down or speeding up the pace.

Once past the opening paragraph — the key in the lock to this house of history and wonders I'm about to explore — the outline usually grows rapidly.

Each time I introduce a character, I take a moment to do a very short bio in the proper document.

Each time I set a scene I make a similar note locating it in a word map of the building, city or countryside. For instance, in my books about Chicago I like to know what parish, political ward and police district the building, house or street corner is in, even if I intend to fictionalize the locality for some reason or other.

Often I set down in the proper document historical milestones that I may or may not include in the text but that will give me a context in which to have my characters operate and live.

I also keep a running record of how much time has transpired in each chapter, whether the book encompasses a day, a month, a year or a decade.

I have a program that prints out calendars for every year for some decades in the past and some years into the future.

I print out the years and months encompassed in my story and mark the principal events of the book on them, accurately matching the day and date.

The notebook stands ready to receive little flashes and notions that will get lost forever in the heat of writing if memory alone is depended upon.

The document for each character's agenda grows in the same organic way.

All of that is largely recordkeeping.

At no time is anything considered engraved in stone. The whole idea is to remain flexible, closing off few options.

The flexibility of the system reveals itself in another way.

As I write I will have the thought that an object mentioned on page four may well be useful for the resolution of a problem, or even the central mystery itself, much farther along in the book. It may even be potentially important enough to bear notice once or twice before the denouement. Moving along the outline I make a notation of those places.

It may be that something about a character deserves development so that the character unfolds and changes before the reader's eyes rather than being offered all of a piece. Such opportunities become part of the expanding outline.

In the book I'm now working on, a character who is afraid of guns is given a political appointment in the sheriff's department in a job where a gun is not required. He places the gun that has been issued to him in a tin box and hides it on the top shelf of his closet. I had no specific intention of using that gun again but not only might it figure in the accident that forces his medical retirement but might even later be used in the commission of a murder by his son. In the final polish, if I decide that there was no need for the gun I might simply leave it there as a character note or take it out altogether as being of no consequence.

I find that characters and situations suggest themselves as I work along. There is a theory of dramaturgy that has to do with the economy of the stage. That is to say: You don't want to create a character whose only reason for being is to walk on and deliver a single piece of information if another character already on the scene can do the job as well.

But at this stage of my novel I don't worry about such considerations. I just pop the characters in there. Later on, if they don't prove to have any purpose or function other than the small bits that thrust them onstage in the first place, I can easily give their lines to some other character and erase them altogether, or I might hold them in reserve as long as their continued presence doesn't distort the shape of the growing outline and narrative.

I find that by the time I'm a hundred pages into a 400-page book, I have fleshed out a credible plot and have a very good idea of how I will proceed, what dangers to my protagonists will appear along the way, what villainies will impede their progress, and I even have a better than fair notion about who the killer will prove to be — if the book is a standard mystery — or how the book will end — if it is a book that doesn't require the classic revelations.

I have discovered through the years, and even now, that retyping pages over and over again to rewrite a paragraph or even a phrase is no longer required. Rereading the work over and over again to refresh my memory of the details and nuances that do not find their way into the outline or the supporting documents, creates a condition in which the words become shopworn and the sinews of the plot are no longer a wonder of literary architecture but merely a cloth riddled with holes.

There's danger here of making changes not because they are better but merely because they are different and I have developed a craving for something green.

So, after each chapter is completed, I use the cut and paste function of my program and create a condensed version of it. Usually the first paragraph and the last, with a few significant paragraphs in between.

Then, when I want and need to get the threads of the story refreshed in my mind before the new day's writing session, I read the brief version, which is usually more than enough to do the job.

Of course the book will have to be read in its entirety more than once while it is in progress, but three or four readings instead of twelve or fifteen will keep it from going stale too soon.

Obviously this process of outlining might be done in the conventional way, thinking everything through and setting the scenes and characters down before the actual finished work is begun. But I find that by walking alongside my characters before they are fully formed I'm often pleasantly, even dramatically, surprised by conversations, actions and philosophies that I could not have imagined. When deep into a scene, writing on overdrive as it were, something magical very often takes place, some hidden well of imagination tapped, and I find myself a passenger floating on the raft of what is sometimes called inspiration along a river of words in full flood.

Before I became a writer I was a painter. When in art school, we were told to go to museums and paint reproductions of the old and new masters.

It was astonishing how much could be learned in the process. In learning how to achieve results similar to those in those skillful paintings, the student learned how color worked, how complements properly mixed with black and white produced an extraordinary range of grays. We learned how to achieve certain textures, the richness of wool and the slickness of satin, by edge and highlight control. We saw that shadows contain the complement of the source of the light. But most of all, I think, we learned the conversation of painting, the interaction of one corner of the canvas with another, the far distance with the near distance, this color and value and texture against others.

So I suggest that you occasionally spend some time studying the anatomy of books you admire, breaking them apart into an outline and ancillary documents such as I have described. This method, like all writing methods, is an attempt to make a writer's life a little easier, a little more orderly. It may not be the best method for you, but I think that by altering and refining it to suit your writing temperament you may fashion procedures that will work best for you.

CHAPTER 14

WHICH VIEWPOINT, AND WHY

MAX BYRD

The most important decision a novelist makes is whether to write in the first or third person.

When I began *Target of Opportunity*, it was to be the fourth novel in my series about Mike Haller, the hard-boiled, eggheaded private detective I had described to myself as "the grandson of Philip Marlowe," a character I had grown fond of, a comfortable old shoe of a voice.

My editor said no.

She read a few chapters of the new manuscript, then called me to say that by now the voice was *too* comfortable, the private eye formula routine. She wanted me to break out of the detective genre and try to write a bigger, more ambitious book. And, unlike my earlier novels, she wanted this one to be written in the third person.

For a month or so I attempted to cooperate and still stay comfortable. I rewrote all of my new chapters, seventy pages or so, simply altering Mike Haller's conventional first person to an objective, neutral third-person narrative: "He said" for "I said." But it didn't need another phone call from the editor to convince me that this approach wasn't working. What was gained by my substituting neutrality and objectivity for a characteristic human voice? Who would want to read it? I was rearranging my formula, but I wasn't creating something new. To write in the third person, I had to admit, meant writing in a completely different way, with completely different characters. As things turned out, it also meant solving a problem of plotting that up until then had seemed to me unsolvable.

The advantages of first person are easy to see — directness, intensity, ease, naturalness. It was no accident, I told myself, that the very first English novelist, Daniel Defoe, had turned instinctively to first-person narration: All of his characters tell their stories in distinctive, confessional voices. Robinson Crusoe recounts his own "life and surprising adventures"; Moll Flanders tallies up husbands, lovers, thefts and bankruptcies on her own nimble fingers. Even the eighteenth-century novelists who had come immediately after Defoe followed his example. The epistolary novels of Samuel Richardson, for example, including his great tragic masterpiece *Clarissa*, were all variations of the first-person technique Defoe had pioneered. Through his device of conflicting letters from many different characters, Richardson achieved a wider scale and point of view than Defoe, each letter writer telling his story in the first person. Richardson himself peeps up occasionally as "editor" of the letters, a mild voice from the prompter's box, barely audible against the actors onstage.

When I looked at my shelf of detective novels, I saw that a disproportionate number of those I admire were in autobiographical first person: Dick Francis, Raymond Chandler, Ross MacDonald, Robert Parker. None of them had apparently even tried third person. And understandably enough: In the classic detective story, the detective is always a kind of surrogate novelist; his job, like the novelist's, is to understand the characters perfectly and to tell and retell the plot until it comes out right. His voice is the voice of the writer himself, projected onto the screen of the blank page.

This, when I thought about it, was the greatest advantage of first-person narration, the reason beginning writers are urged (rightly) to use it. There is no quicker, surer way to your own feelings. The person who writes: "*I* said . . ." "*I* did . . ." "*I* wanted . . ." for 300 pages is unavoidably writing about himself, drawing consciously or unconsciously on his own personality for material, then re-creating that personality, however distorted by plot, in the story he writes. First-person writing is ventriloquism. It's no surprise that steeplechase jockey Dick Francis, who was thrown violently from so many horses, writes so often and so powerfully about physical pain; or that Lew Archer expresses in every dark metaphor the wise *tristesse* that Ross MacDonald always communicated in real life; or that Philip Marlowe turns so often to the bottle that Raymond Chandler kept in his desk drawer.

But with all this in mind I still remembered my editor's admonition that Henry James — she had rolled out the big guns — believed no writer achieved the level of *art* as opposed to autobiography until he mastered the third person. And so I set out to write *Target of Opportunity* as a brand-new story.

Two things I gave up at once: the character of Mike Haller and nearly the same thing — Mike Haller's *style*, his wisecracking, Marlow-esque, conventionally ironic way of talking. Three things I saw I had gained:

1. Scale. Third-person narration permitted a grand expansion of geographic scale. The book was to be set in many distant places: London, the English countryside, the Dordogne Valley of southwestern France in 1944, San Francisco, Lake Tahoe, Boston today. With a cinematic flick of the eye, while Mike Haller was still slowly boarding a plane, third person could change cities or even continents. For a moment, I felt like a lordly Ludlum or Forsyth, studying my novel as if it were a huge map of the world, moving my characters effortlessly across it like plastic models.

2. I had gained flexibility of subplot. In first-person narration, any subplot necessarily has to involve the narrator, sometimes as observer, more frequently as participant: He must be on the spot when the subplot starts rolling. In most cases, this limitation means that the subplot of an action novel has to be a romance: When not busy solving the crime, the hero or heroine has to be falling in or out of love (this works to perfection in such novels as Dick Francis's *Whip Hand* or Chandler's *Long Goodbye*). But a larger, more complete effect comes about when the subplot *independently* reflects the themes of the main action, as Gloucester's tribulations with his sons reflect King Lears' with his daughters. For the first time my plot and subplot could hold mirrors up to each other: The secondary theme I had chosen of fathers and sons at war in present-day America would reflect fathers and sons at war in 1944.

3. I had also gained a wider cast of characters. Elmore Leonard has noted that in every book he writes some minor character unexpectedly grows to importance or even threatens to take over the whole story. But of course a writer needs to be free to let these characters perform. In *Target of Opportunity*, I suddenly found that I could wheel the spotlight wherever I wanted. To give only one example, nothing makes a character seem more realistic than giving him or her strong, habitual likes and dislikes, especially in small things; they push the character back in time, forward into the future, they give him depth. In first person, it is easy enough for the narrator to reveal that from childhood on he has hated the smell of coffee or loved women with freckled noses, but it is frequently awkward for other characters to say such things to the narrator. By contrast, the third-person voice can swoop in and out of any character's mind, like a bird through an open window, observing everything, bringing everything back. Here is John Le Carre building two characters at once in *The Little Drummer Girl*, letting Kurtz's habitual impatience with detail play against Lenny's goodness:

> Lenny was big-hearted and kind, but a little shy of people he was not observing. He had wide ears and an ugly, over-featured face, and perhaps that was why he kept it from the hard gaze of the world. . . . In other circumstances Kurtz could tire of detail very quickly, but he respected Lenny and paid the closest attention to everything he said, nodding, congratulating, making all the right expressions for him.

With these "gains," I had, however, also raised an unexpected question: In third person, how loud is the narrator's voice to be? In first-person narration, there is never a difficulty about point of view or voice: It is always the narrator speaking, even if he tells somebody else's story. But in third-person narration, do you look over every character's shoulder? or only one?

Most writers decide on multiple points of view, either alternating them in chapters or larger sections (as I chose to do), or darting back and forth on the same page as Elmore Leonard does. Curiously, Martin Cruz Smith's marvelous novel *Gorky Park* takes the point of view of only one person — the Moscow policeman Arkady — yet sticks to the third person. The advantages Smith gains are subtle but strong: Typically he begins a chapter with no more than a sentence or two of capsule biography/description ("She had a broad, child's face, innocent blue eyes, a narrow waist and small breasts with nipples as tiny as vaccination marks.") More frequently, he begins with a paragraph of setting:

> Almost all Russia is old, graded by glaciers that left a landscape of low hills, lakes and rivers that wander like the trails of worms in soft wood. North of the city, Silver Lake

was frozen, and all the summer dachas on the lake were deserted, except Iamskoy's.

At which point he smoothly moves his protagonist in front of the picture ("Arkady parked behind a Chaika limousine"), so that the effect is of seeing these things through Arkady's mind, though they are rarely things he would have thought or known. And this is all the more important because a major strength of Smith's book is the knowledge it gives us of an exotic land, the encyclopedic, wide-screen effect of scale it creates, even while its focus stays tightly on Arkady's actions.

For *Target of Opportunity* I lacked (among many other talents) Smith's gift for linking geographic scale and individual character. But I noticed that many of his preliminary settings did what my notion of habitual likes and dislikes did: They established a depth of time, geological and historical, that lent still more realism to his fictional world. A third-person narrative, I realized, was free to manipulate *time* as well as place. And with that realization my unsolvable problem of plot was solved.

My original plan had been to have a plot in which, as I pictured it, two parallels meet. That is, I wanted to draw on the detective story premise as old as at least Sophocles: *There is always an earlier crime.* The present crime is always explained by discovering the crime that has provoked it, so my protagonist was to solve a present crime in Boston by uncovering an earlier crime in the French Resistance, some forty years before. When writing a first-person Mike Haller novel, I saw no easy way to describe those events of 1944. Haller obviously couldn't be there. I might have someone *tell* him about it, or he might find an incriminating diary or letter, but these seemed very mechanical devices and likely to work only with a good deal of creaking. Third-person narration, however, would allow me to set my two story lines down independently. I could simply start with the enigmatic scenes of 1944 — write what amounted to fifty pages of historical fiction, something I had never done before — and then let those scenes collide in the reader's imagination with contemporary events in Boston. The past was a bullet aimed at the present. Past and present would intersect explosively. Individual lives would gain scale and depth because their courses had been set long ago, fatally, by the great war. History was destiny.

To my surprise, third-person narration had not only solved my technical problem, it had also revealed my basic theme.

CHAPTER 15

DRESS FOR SUCCESS: YOUR PERSONAL STYLE

CAROLYN WHEAT

What is style? Is it something a writer can consciously enhance, or is it a mystical quantum leap that comes only after years of writing effort? Is it layering of metaphors, juggling images, reaching for abstruse adjectives, decorating a wedding cake of words? Or is it the laconic "just the facts, ma'am" prose made popular by Ernest Hemingway, Dashiell Hammett and Joe Friday?

What is style? And how can I get one?

John Gardner says "fiction is like a dream." Style creates that dream, keeping the reader's eyes glued to the page, hoisting him astride a steeplechase jumper along with Dick Francis's hero or causing her heart to pound as Kinsey Millhone tracks a killer. Style adds texture, gives life to two-dimensional words strung along a blank white page.

We know style when we see it. It's as effortless as Astaire's dancing, as appropriate as black at a funeral, as organic as a mulch-grown tomato. We smile with recognition at a well-turned phrase; our pulses race as action verbs hurtle us along a roller coaster of suspense.

We know bad style too. Maybe not consciously, but that book we put down and never picked up again probably had flat prose, talk-alike characters, or (on the flip side) forced metaphors, florid adjectives, judgmental writing that kept us from becoming enveloped by the fictional dream.

Style is to prose exactly what it is to fashion. We choose one set of clothes to wear to a job interview, another to climb Pike's Peak. Our clothes serve a purpose, whether our object is to impress a prospective employer, or to stay comfortable on a strenuous trail. We choose colors, fabrics, styles that say something about who we are. Our prose reflects our personality, too, whether consciously or unconsciously.

That's what style is. Now, how do we get one?

First, don't think about it. Just write the story. Let the events happen and the characters make their moves and speak their lines. Tell your story simply, the way you'd describe a movie to a friend who hasn't seen it yet.

Your early chapters will be a mishmash of styles. You're writing your way into the story. Some passages will be too long, as you grope for the essence of a character. There'll be boring passages, as you concentrate on getting the story on paper. You'll probably write a few purple paragraphs, as you imitate the style of the latest best-seller.

Your early chapters may look like a schizophrenic's closet, with nothing quite matching anything else.

Don't worry.

Somewhere around the first third to half of your novel, a style will begin to emerge, shy as a kitten at first, creeping onto the page almost unnoticed. This happened to a friend of mine, who was writing an atmospheric suspense novel set in Maine. The early chapters were good, but uneven. Around the sixth month of work, the book suddenly took on *style*. Metaphors of the sea, of foggy nights, of waves crashing on rocky shores abounded. The outer world of the story reflected the characters' inner mood in a wholly natural way. The rest of the book flowed, the style deepening the atmosphere the author was striving to create. She was making the dream happen.

As my friend said later, style was simply a matter of making the book *exactly* what she had always wanted it to be — a haunting tale large on atmosphere. She just hadn't known that when she started writing.

Problem: what about those early chapters, the ones with choppy style, the lifeless passages, the fat? Answer: rewrite, rewrite, rewrite. Empty that closet of anything that doesn't fit the image you've chosen for your book. Pare down that wardrobe and concentrate on quality. You *have* your style now, the one that's perfect for this book. All you have to do is recast the opening chapters in the same mode.

Suppose you're not writing for atmosphere, but for suspense? Suppose you're writing a classic puzzle mystery? How do you know what style is appropriate for the book you want to create?

The writer whose vision is a gritty, street-smart, hard-boiled story can do no better than to study Lawrence Sanders (*The Timothy Game*):

> It's a peppy August day, which does nothing for his crusty mood. So the sun is shining. Big deal. That's what it's getting paid for, isn't it?

> Cone plods down Broadway to Exchange Place. It's a spiffy day with lots of sunshine, washed sky, and a smacking breeze. Streets of the financial district are crowded, everyone hurries, the pursuit of the Great Simoleon continuing with vigor and determination.

How many descriptions of how many "nice days" have you skimmed in your reading life? How many have been this "spiffy," this connected to the personality of the narrator, this good at contrasting nature with "the pursuit of the Great Simoleon"? We're talking style here, style that puts us smack into the character's mood and leaves us wanting more. This guy grabs all our attention just walking down the street.

Style serves a purpose. An action book needs an active style, with short sentences, punchy verbs. Here's T. Jefferson Parker in *Little Saigon*:

> Cops were all over the Asian Wind. Light bars pulsed, flashing against the building. Radios squawked. Two officers strung yellow crime-scene tape between sawhorses. An ambulance sped away.

The author evokes the controlled chaos of crime-scene cops in five—count them, five—well-chosen sentences. Another writer could have taken five paragraphs to say the same thing.

And maybe that mythical other writer *needs* five paragraphs. Maybe he's writing, not a suspense thriller where the cops are walk-ons, but a police procedural in which every detail of crime-scene protocol will be elaborated for the reader. Parker's purpose is to keep the story moving, and to get the cops on and offstage quickly. His style fits his purpose. The procedural writer's style will do the same thing, only differently. For him, the police are central to the story. What they do, how they do it, what they talk about while they're doing it will be central to his vision, and therefore worthy of five paragraphs, or even five pages.

What about classic "mystery" style? Robert Barnard has written of Agatha Christie that her "talent to deceive" often displayed itself through a deceptively "ordinary" prose style. If you know who killed Roger Ackroyd, the following sentence will be rich with subtle meaning. In it, the book's narrator tells the reader that he has had a conversation with Hercule Poirot. Note the italicized words (*The Murder of Roger Ackroyd*):

> *Thus enjoined*, I plunged into a *careful* narrative, embodying all the facts *I have previously set down*.

To the reader who doesn't know who killed Roger Ackroyd, the sentence is simple, even boring. A man tells us (the readers) that he has given Poirot "a careful narrative." He saves us time by telling us that he told Poirot "all the facts I have previously set down," without bothering to repeat them.

As Barnard says, what Christie knew as a mystery writer was How People Read Books. We go for the high spots; our eyes glide over sentences like the one quoted above. Only later (and maybe not even then) do we realize that in that spare line of narrative Significant Clues lie buried.

Simple words move us more than high-flown language. In *A Prey to Murder*, Ann Cleeves's amateur sleuth explains why he is driven to solve the murder of an old friend:

> He had always thought revenge a misguided and destructive emotion, but having seen Eleanor lying on the grass amid the droppings, the dirty straw, the discarded pieces of fur and feather of the birds' prey, he felt angry and violent. She was beautiful, he had admired her, and she had been killed.

Note "the rule of three" in the last sentence — three simple phrases, strung together, which add up to a powerful motive. Note also that each of the three phrases holds up a different facet of the narrator's mood. Too many new writers use the "rule of three" as a vehicle for repeating the same idea three different ways: "He was tired as a bear in winter, exhausted as a car out of gas, as limp as an old dishcloth." This dissipates the point rather than builds it. Pick one image that conveys "tiredness" as strongly as you want it to, and stop there.

Great style is organic. It doesn't reach, but uses the materials ready at hand. Here's T. Jefferson Parker again, describing his detective/hero (*Little Saigon*):

> It was, in fact, a cave-house—with back rooms being nothing more than dark irregular caverns. But the living room, bedroom, kitchen and bath featured walls, electricity, and unimpeded views of the Pacific. *Frye's friends said that the cave-house was like Frye himself: half-finished, prone to dark recesses.*

Was that paragraph in the first draft? Did Parker see his hero from the first in terms of his cave-house? Maybe—but my personal guess is that the description came later, as the character revealed himself to his author, as the revision process brought the finished style out of the cave of the first draft. In any case, the passage works because it comes straight from the elements of the story.

Metaphor is a great aid to style, but only if the metaphors arise from the context instead of being foreign "literary" elements tacked on without relevance. A writer friend says of metaphors that they must be both true and surprising. How to achieve this happy end? Try looking at your story elements the way Parker looked at Frye's cave-house. How does your hero(ine) view the world? With the self-deprecating humor of a Lovejoy, or the Victorian pessimism of Anne Perry's Inspector Pitt? Let those elements creep into the writing.

Dr. Matilda Flint, "Dr. Mattie" to the many fans of Roy Sorrels's mini-mysteries, is a general practitioner whose small town has a murder rate to rival that of Cabot's Cove, Maine. Her voice is all her own, as the opening lines of "Message for Dr. Mattie" demonstrate:

> There I was, sitting in my recliner chair counting cricket chirps. Now, before you go thinking the butter's slipped off my noodles, let me establish my credentials. Dr. Matilda Flint's my name, but folks in our town call me Dr. Mattie and have for half a century or so. I'm 75 years old, and although some mornings in winter I feel old as coal when I creak out of bed, for the most part, I'm of sound mind and body.

Two elements aid the style here: the "true and surprising" metaphor *as old as coal*, and the newly minted image for senility, *the butter's slipped off my noodles.*

Going for an attention-getter works especially well in the opening of a book or chapter. Here's Roger L. Simon (*California Roll*):

> I never sold out before because nobody ever asked me.

Try for contrasts — like the sunny day vs. Timothy Cone's mood. Contrast long vs. short sentences, flowery images vs. plain talk, scenes vs. narrative.

When writing suspense/action, nothing says more than vivid verbs, sense-oriented adjectives. You're putting the reader into the dream — or is it the nightmare? — with a vengeance (*A Stranger Is Watching*, Mary Higgins Clark):

> It was no use, no use, no use. Her eyes magnetized by the clock, Sharon frantically tried to jab the broken edge of the handle into the cords of her wrists. . . .
>
> More times than not, she missed the cords completely and the metal cut into her hand. She could feel the warm, soft, sticky blood, running, crusting.
>
> Leaning on her left elbow, Sharon dragged herself up. She swung just enough to support her back against the wall and managed to squirm to a sitting position. Her legs fell over the side of the cot. Raw pain screeched through her ankle.

Note the repetition of the first three lines, the graphic description of the blood, the use of verbs like "jab," "dragged," "squirm," and "screeched." With every move Sharon makes, we the readers move with her, feeling her agony, almost smelling the blood.

Put spin on the ball by varying well-known clichés. Archie Goodwin describes a woman baring her soul to Nero Wolfe (*Black Orchids*, Rex Stout):

> The seams had ripped and the beans were tumbling out,
> and Wolfe sat back and let them come.

That's a lot zippier than saying, "She spilled the beans," isn't it?

Beware of judgmental writing. How many otherwise good writers tell a story (even in first person) with so many opinions on the page that the reader feels manipulated, told what to think and how to feel? Good, pithy description is a hallmark of mystery-thriller writing, but its downside is a tendency to sum people up too quickly. Here's how Lawrence Sanders does it in *The Timothy Game*:

> She's a big, florid woman with shards of great beauty. But it's all gone to puff now. It could be the sauce, but Cone reckons that's only a symptom, not the malady. Thwarted ambitions, soured dreams, chilled loves—all came before the booze. Now her life is tottering, ready to fall. It's there in her glazed eyes and sappy grin.

What saves this passage from judgmentalism is the obvious compassion Timothy Cone feels for this woman. It helps that he gives us specific details supporting his conclusion—the glazed eyes, the sappy grin. He doesn't just sum her up as "a lush" and dismiss her.

Beware of copyeditors. Copyeditors are great people who know where the commas ought to go and how to spell *oleaginous*. They are also good at pointing out that on page twenty-four the doorman had on a blue uniform, whereas on page eighty he'd switched to gray. We need copyeditors.

They do not, however, appreciate style. They opt invariably for the bland, the predictable, the done-before. If their suggestions—and that's all they will be, suggestions—flatten your prose and take the spice out of your chili, RESIST. Your personal style is just that—personal.

Beware of what you do best. This is a toughie. You write the meanest metaphor on the block. Your dialogue snaps, crackles, and pops. Your descriptions are sheer poetry. So you use your strong points over, and over, and over again.

Like the man said, kill your darlings. Not all of them, just the ones that clog up the story, murder true style by showing off, and kill the dream by reducing it to a bunch of words on a page.

CHAPTER 16

How to Write Convincing Dialogue

Aaron Elkins

How-to books on mystery writing are nothing new. They've been around since *The Technique of the Mystery Story* was put out by The Home Correspondence School in 1913. The 1929 revision of this estimable volume consists of 435 pages of sound professional advice. There are 153 titled chapters or sections ranging from "Devious Devices" and "Remarkable Deductions From Footprints," to "Need Love Be Excluded?" and "What Else to Eschew."

Not one refers to dialogue, even indirectly.

Neither do the 500-plus entries in the index. The average mystery writer of sixty years ago, with a few towering exceptions, simply didn't worry overmuch about dialogue. Or characterization. Or setting. (Nope, those aren't in the index either.) A mystery novel, or a detective story as it was then more often called, was first and last a matter of ingenious plotting.

Well, things have changed. A good plot is no longer enough. Unless it's acted out by plausible, rounded characters convincingly portrayed, it's not going to make it with today's readers. And when it comes to creating believeable characters, nothing serves better and more straight-forwardly than dialogue, which is, after all, your characters' only opportunity to speak for themselves. On the other hand, nothing will alienate, bore, and irritate readers faster than dubious, badly written dialogue.

Here then are some thoughts and cautions on the enjoyable, fascinating, treacherous craft of dialogue writing.

Speaking in Voices

A character's voice is the distinctive way he or she speaks: vocabulary, cadence, tempo, slang, subject matter, tone and any other aspect of speech. Voice is the most direct way we have to flesh out our characters. In my own writing, one of the last passes I make through a manuscript is to review the dialogue sections to make sure that every line of speech seems right — that is, consistent — for the speaker. Is this the way Tony would answer that question, or does it sound too much like Ben? Would Anne really express anger like that? If not, what's wrong with it? How do I fix it? The point is, if I can't distinguish between the way my people talk, how can I expect my readers to?

Some writers' guides recommend that you differentiate your characters' speech patterns by assigning "types": having one character who speaks formally, another who's laconic, another who's meticulous, etc., and then making sure that you stick to that type when you write dialogue for them.

Personally, I don't think it's a good idea. People who respond predictably are tedious in real life and more so in books. What I usually do instead is model my characters' speech on that of real people — usually acquaintances (who never recognize themselves, by the way) or other people I've spent time observing personally, but often familiar public figures too. The question then becomes: Is this the way Dan Quayle — or Margaret Thatcher, or Cher, or Vince at the Safeway store — would probably say this? It's relatively easy, it develops the ear, and it's downright enjoyable.

It's Not What They Say, It's How They Say It

Most mysteries require a lot of talk. Complex information has to be brought out, and dialogue is often the best or even the only way to do it. Someone, most often the protagonist, asks questions . . . Who? Why?

Where? . . . and someone answers. It's certainly efficient, but nothing is likely to put a reader to sleep quicker (or more deeply) than paragraph on paragraph of dialogue establishing dates, times, places and prior events.

How do you avoid this and still present the needed data? You grit your teeth, gird your loins, and sit down and force content-heavy dialogue to do double or even triple duty. Can the conversation itself, aside from the necessary content, fill in important aspects of character, develop mood, reveal significant motives and perceptions? Ruth Rendell is a past master at this. Here is an early passage from *The Veiled One*.

> "Yes, I go to Serge Olson. It's a sort of Jungian therapy he does. Do you want his address?"
>
> Burden nodded, noted it down. "May I ask why you go to . . . Dr. Olson, is it?"
>
> Clifford, who showed no signs of the cold his mother claimed for him, was looking at the mirror but not into it. Burden would have sworn he was not seeing his own reflection. "I need help," he said.
>
> Something about the rigidity of his figure, his stillness and the dullness of his eyes stopped Burden pursuing this. Instead he asked if Clifford had been to the psychotherapist on Thursday afternoon and what time he had left.
>
> "It's an hour I go for, five till six. My mother told me you knew I was in the car park—I mean, that I put the car there."
>
> "Yes. Why didn't you tell us that at first?"
>
> He shifted his eyes, not to Burden's face but to the middle of his chest. And when he answered Burden recognized the phraseology, the manner of speech, as that which people in therapy—no matter how inhibited, reserved, disturbed—inevitably pick up. He had heard it before. "I felt threatened."
>
> "By what?"
>
> "I'd like to talk to Serge now. If I'd had some sort of warning I'd have tried to make an appointment with him and talk it through with him."
>
> "I'm afraid you're going to have to make do with me, Mr. Sanders."

The essential data—time and place—are established, but how much more than that she tells us about the two people.

Move It Right Along, Please

For most of us, writing dialogue is fun, at least when it's rolling effortlessly along, which is precisely when it tends to get away from us. I wouldn't want to count the number of times I've had to delete five or six pages of dialogue—two or three days' work—not because it was badly written, but because I'd gotten off on a tangent that didn't take the story anywhere.

In some kinds of fiction this might be all right, but in the mystery you'd better keep that story moving along if you hope to keep your readers. When they start flipping ahead to get to the next place where something happens, you're in trouble. And they *will* start flipping if they sense that the plot's been put on idle. Fortunately you can sense it too if you read your own material with care. No matter how much wonderful mood or character development a dialogue scene may be providing, it has to get your story someplace. If it doesn't, then cut it, painful as it may be.

Sometimes, in fact, a scalpel-like approach to dialogue is in itself a tool for moving a story jauntily along. Here's an example from a book of mine called *Murder in the Queen's Armes*. The scene is a village museum in England from which a fossilized skull fragment of Poundsbury Man (familiarly, Pummy) has disappeared.

> Professor Hall-Waddington thrust his face into the box. "Empty! Pummy . . . Pummy appears to have been . . ." He held the box in trembling hands and looked up at Gideon with wondering eyes. "But why would anyone steal a thirty-thousand-year-old parieto-occipital calvareal fragment?"

End of chapter one. I know, this may not be the kind of crisis that makes you clench your teeth with tension, but it does provide a nice, sharp close, right at the climactic moment, to an exchange that might otherwise have petered slowly out. It also ends the chapter with a question, always a nice idea for prodding a reader into turning the page.

And how does chapter two begin? This way:

> "Why *would* anyone steal a thirty-thousand-year-old whatzit?" Julie asked, her black eyes no less wondering.
> "Beats the hell out of me," Gideon said.

The dialogue begins as cleanly as it left off. And in so doing that wearisome bugbear of writers new and old—the transition from one scene to another—is sidestepped. No tiresome "After leaving Professor Hall-

Waddington, Gideon walked thoughtfully along the High Street to the little park where he was to meet . . ." The new scene takes off from the old one, jumpstarted, so to speak, and in the doing there is even an opportunity for a little character development.

"... ," He Ululated Menacingly

New writers seem to worry a lot — probably too much — about how often you can get away with writing "he said," or "she said." There are two opposing schools of thought on this. One, subscribed to by some of the greatest writers in the English language, affirms that "said" is the only verb of attribution needed to identify who is speaking. The other school considers "said" colorless, preferring more spirited words like "mocked," "bleated," "gritted," "rasped," "ground out," and "hissed." This school is heavily represented in the formula romance racks of your supermarket.

Fortunately there is a sensible intermediate position, (which I just happen to hold). I think that "said" functions very well indeed as the writer's standby, but that a little variety is not to be sneered at. There are other good speech-descriptors too, all with their own nuances of meaning. "Asked," "explained," "mused," "noted," "whispered," "cried," "repeated," "shouted," "told," and "informed" are examples of perfectly good variants, as long as they aren't used so excessively that they catch the reader's eye and thus disrupt the flow of the story. How much is "excessively"? My own rule of thumb is no more than once a chapter for any one of them. If I find two "whispered"s in a single chapter, I usually replace one with "said."

There are other ways around the problem. An obvious one is to use fewer verbs of attribution altogether. A brief conversation between two people needs no more than a single "he said" or "she said" at the beginning to establish who is speaking. Longer dialogues can get by just fine with one every fifth or sixth time the speaker changes. And question-and-answer sessions, as in courtroom scenes or interrogations, can go on for twenty pages without a "he said" and still be completely clear as to who's doing the talking.

Ramona Sipped Her Strawberry Daiquiri, (Toyed with her wedding band — pondered the alternatives — lifted an eyebrow imperceptibly) "Really, Darling ..."

Another way to avoid an overabundance of verbs of attribution, and to enliven scenes as well, is to identify the speaker by action or thought, as in the following exchange:

"Look, I wasn't even in Omaha last Wednesday." Lester stared sullenly at the paint-spattered floor.

"Is that right?" Walter smiled pleasantly. "I'm afraid I don't believe that."

Neither did Vincent. "Where, then?"

If you want to find examples of fine dialogue writing that goes on for pages without using a single "said," read some Robert Barnard. On the other hand, if you need confirmation that one can write riveting dialogue while relying on nothing but "said," try a Tony Hillerman.

While we're on the subject, still another way to eliminate verbs of attribution and also speed things up is to slip out of the dialogue mode for as long as necessary, then pick up the dialogue again when you're ready. Do it well, and the reader will never notice. This is an example from *The Killing Zone* by Rex Burns:

> "What was his schedule for Wednesday?"
>
> She told him, pointing to the calendar and explaining its abbreviations. In addition to routine committee work, meetings, and functions, he had a dozen-or-so visitors to talk to.
>
> "Is that usual?"

A lot of dull, nonessential material was deftly slipped by us there, without missing a beat.

Veracity Vs. Verisimilitude

"You know how, how . . . but . . . some mornings the minute you walk in the door—"

"Every morning."

"Yes, that's how these, the way they, the way they . . ."

"No, it's not. It's not the, the—"

"Yes, it is, it is. Because if you, unless you—"

"No, uh-uh, absolutely not."

Absolutely not what? What are they talking about? Would you keep reading a book with dialogue like that? Neither would I. Yet this is a snatch of authentic dialogue, the speech of real people; two intelligent, literate women engaged in an earnest discussion. I scribbled it down verbatim a few mornings ago on a Seattle-bound commuter ferry. Suppose that the next day I'd given them pens and asked them to write down their entire half-hour conversation. Would this particular passage show up?

Not a chance. People may talk that way, but they don't remember it that way. Which takes me to a critical point. Every mystery writer had better be concerned about writing realistic dialogue — but "realistic" isn't the same thing as "real." In writing realistic dialogue we're not trying to document authentic speech, we're trying to set it down as people remember speech, as they think it ought to have been. Genuine or not, a conversational passage like the one above has no place in mystery fiction unless it's there to make a point. Even then, it better not go on very long.

Realistic dialogue attempts to capture the flavor of real speech, but it does it selectively. Word repetitions, hesitations, stammers and dead ends have to be ruthlessly pruned. So do many of the polite conventions.

"Hey, come on in, Hal, glad you made it. Care for a drink? Scotch? Coffee? Why don't you sit right there, Hal?"

In real life people do a lot of this. That's fine for them; they're not living out somebody's plot and trying to do it in 90,000 words or less. But your characters are. Everything they do — and most emphatically everything they say — must have a point, must take the story somewhere. Otherwise, out with it.

What Else to Eschew

Writing manuals are agreed in their advice on how to use dialect: Don't.

Generally speaking, I agree. There is little that is more awful to the sensitive and discriminating eye than clumsily done dialect, whether foreign — "Vat you vant, meesus?" — or regional — "Ah shore am hongry, chile, cuz ah hain't et mah grits." Dialect in your fiction is likely to make an enemy of your copyeditor and strain the patience of your audience, two things I don't recommend.

Still . . .

It can be done and done well. You don't have to traumatize the language to provide a flavor of foreign or regional speech. Sometimes a few simple adjustments will suffice. For example, an inoffensive sort of all-purpose foreign accent can be achieved simply by eliminating the use of contractions.

"Now, we'll see what's going to happen" sounds like an American speaking. But "Now we will see what is going to happen" sounds to most of us like a German. Or Frenchman. Or Russian. It works because we know, even if we've never consciously noticed it, that many people who learn English as a foreign language never become comfortable with its frequent use of contractions.

You can dig deeper and show dialects through rhythm, vocabulary and syntax. Here is a typical passage from Stuart Kaminsky's *A Cold Red Sunrise*:

> "What do you want?" Rutkin said.
>
> The creature said nothing.
>
> "Are you drunk?" Rutkin went on. "I am a Soviet Commissar. I am conducting an important investigation and you, you are in my way."
>
> The creature did move now. It moved toward Illya Rutkin, who stepped back, clutching his briefcase protectively to his chest.
>
> "What do you want?" Rutkin shouted. "You want trouble? You want trouble? That can be arranged."

Not a mutilated word in there; no *nyet's* or *da's* either, but Kaminsky, with his good ear, shows Rutkin talking in a way that fits our notion of what a Russian would speak like (if he were speaking Russian in English, of course).

And what if you don't have a good ear? Then go to the language section of your library or a school language deparment and get help. And if you still feel insecure about it? Then give it up. Just write:

"I am Sigurd Asbjornsen," he said, his Norwegian accent almost impenetrable.

And let it go at that. It will get you by satisfactorily, it won't make you look silly, and your copyeditor will love you.

I Was Not Moving My Lips

The critical test of dialogue is how well it stands up to being read aloud. There is just no better way to show up awkwardness or artificiality in written speech than trying to say it. Another one of the final passes I make through my manuscripts is a read-the-dialogue-out-loud exercise. It never fails to turn up some spoken lines that seemed fine when I wrote them but that don't work now. I don't always know what's wrong technically; sometimes all I know is that something is "off." But trying it a few different ways — out loud — almost always gives me something better.

Moving your lips while you read is not to be encouraged. Doing it while you write is.

CHAPTER 17

PACING AND SUSPENSE

PHYLLIS A. WHITNEY

The best lesson I've ever received on pacing came to me from Farnsworth Wright, editor of *Weird Tales*. This was several lifetimes ago in Chicago, before I had written a full-length book. The few stories I had sold as a beginning writer were to the pulp magazines. No paperbacks in those days, so we learned in the pulp field.

Weird Tales was an elite member of the pulp group, and highly respected. I had sold them one story, but was having no success with others I'd submitted. Mr. Wright was kind enough to send me a criticism that has forever proved useful to me: I must not try to keep everything at high pitch all the way through a story. Excitement, if too steady, can be as boring as having nothing at all happening.

This was when I first recognized that a reader's attention could be as easily lost by too much, as by too little. There can be a strong buildup to a dramatic scene, after which we must allow for a letdown, a rest, before we start building up all over again. That is what pacing is.

There is another aspect that is worth considering. If a writer piles on endless defeat and discouragement, the reader may find the story too unpleasant to read. The mystery writer is first of all an entertainer. While the main character's course should never be easy, hope can be laced into the action, and there can be small "wins" along the way. Please, Stephen King, don't kill off all the good characters!

For me, suspense is the fun part of writing. It is the game I most like to play—a game that readers are sure to enjoy when it is handled successfully. The development of suspense should affect every phase of our writing.

In my own novels I start first with a setting that I am able to visit. I want a place that will give me fresh and interesting material that will furnish good scenes for a mystery. One needn't always travel to a distant country. If I look at my own home locale with a fresh eye, I'm likely to find just what I need.

In my fourth book (my first adult mystery) I had only to visit Chicago's Loop and get behind the scenes in the window-decorating section of a big department store. There were wonderful mystery settings I could use, the story developed well, and *Red Is for Murder* got good reviews. It sold about 3,000 copies and I decided (with Mystery Writers of America) that crime certainly didn't pay enough. I returned happily to writing for young people—in which field I eventually learned the craft of mystery writing. Years later, when I had been "discovered," my adult mystery was reprinted many times in paper, and is still selling as *The Red Carnelian*. Styles in titles can change. So take heart if your first novel doesn't succeed. Earn your stripes and all the old titles will be reissued.

Once I visit a new background, I look deliberately for scenes that will trigger my imagination. In St. Thomas, Virgin Islands, I immediately noticed the "catchments" on every hillside. These were huge, steep, concrete constructions that caught rainfall and sent the water into containers at the bottom. When I climbed up to see what one of these looked like from the top, my first reaction was, "What a wonderful place for a murder!" So I used a catchment in *Columbella* to good effect. Suspense grows out of our own reactions first of all.

Writer's block is unlikely to occur if we find new experiences and impressions to feed into the creative right brain. Each new place or subject requires library research, and this in itself will provide fresh ideas that we can use.

Once I have my setting, I search for a main character who will be driven to solve a life-or-death problem. Little difficulties don't build high suspense. The more serious and threatening the problem, the higher the reader's interest. No strong drive for the main character will result in a weak story.

We need to think about this powerful drive in our planning stages. It is easier to build this quality into an action story, than into something more quiet. Yet the latter can create just as much page-turning suspense, if the writer remains aware of the character's desperate need to reach an important goal. Taking action needn't always be violent.

In the beginning the main character may not know what action is needed. Sooner or later, however, he or she must decide to *do something*. This is the point where the story really begins. Until this happens, it's all preparation. It is all too easy to mark time and let a character drift along for too many chapters without making a decision to act. He may be caught up in other characters' problems, and the writer may need to pull up short and face what must be done to hold the reader.

Giving my character a purpose — something she must strive for in every scene — not always a major problem, but at least something that will lead into the main goal of the character. Sometimes there may really be a situation in which my heroine can take no action on her own. Then I bring on another character who has a strong drive, and perhaps a very different goal, so that she is forced into taking action. Suspense results.

In any piece of writing we can count on reader curiosity to carry the story for a time. Providing, of course, that we furnish something to be curious about. We need story people who are interesting enough to make readers wonder what they will do next. What are these strange goings-on, and what is this person hiding? Curiosity serves us well in the beginning, and from time to time thereafter.

Long ago, in writing for young people, I learned the value of the eccentric character. These are always fun to do, since they are dramatic, flamboyant, out of the ordinary. Such characters furnish suspense by doing the unexpected and perhaps messing everything up. The reader stays to see what on earth will develop next. It's advisable not to have more than one eccentric character per novel. Overdo this and the reality is lost.

Writing from a single viewpoint happens to be my choice. It isn't always easy to achieve, but I like its special advantages. Most writers seem to prefer the multiple viewpoint, since it enables them to skip around into the minds of various characters. There may be added suspense when the reader knows something the character doesn't, and can see danger coming. One of the handicaps in using different viewpoints lies in the letdown that can result when the reader must leave a character in whom a strong interest has developed, to move to someone unknown, or about whom we may not care. This requires a quick new buildup of interest and suspense, or the reader is likely to put the book aside.

For me, the strong suspense that results from immediacy—that sense of everything happening *now*—is increased when I stay in the thoughts and feelings of one character.

Whether I write in third or first person, emotion can be more readily felt by the reader when I stay in the single viewpoint. Emotion is always an important ingredient. The reader who feels nothing, because the character feels nothing, is quickly bored. We do need to care. Worry and fear can be more intense when we follow the fate of one character. Breaking viewpoints can dilute.

If you do use several viewpoints, however, don't skip around into more than one mind on a page. It's much safer to use one viewpoint per chapter—unless confusion is your aim.

A major objection to the single viewpoint is that the writer may want to show events at which the main character can't be present. I have always found a way around this—perhaps through another character's report, which can be dramatized.

Describing the main character can offer some difficulty in the single viewpoint. We can't step outside and objectively look at this person. Once a pulp editor asked me to stop standing my heroines in front of mirrors. That is certainly a hoary device, yet I'm still guilty at times when it seems appropriate. Working a bit harder, I can usually find ways to give bits of description through other persons in the story who talk to the main character. In my experience the single viewpoint is apt to build intense suspense.

Of course the basic idea of plot must never be forgotten. I bring this up because of my years of experience in working with beginning writers as a teacher. Too often a string of incidents is regarded as a plot. I've often used Forster's example: *The king died and then the queen died.* This is a string of incidents. But if you say, *The king died and then the queen died of grief*, you have a plot. Cause and effect. Whatever happens grows out of what happened before, and results in future happenings.

Another useful element in building suspense is to do the unexpected. If a reader can guess what is going to happen, we lose him. So we push ourselves to discard easy approaches and try to surprise with the astonishing, but logical. In my current writing (*Woman Without a Past*) my main character finds herself alone and abandoned at three in the morning in the dungeon of the Old Exchange Building in Charleston, South Carolina. She has arrived there through surprising, but logical circumstances. There is some suspense, but I needed more. So I even surprised myself. While my heroine is groping her way blindly in the pitch dark among the brick pillars of this echoing place, her outstretched hand rests suddenly on the warm human flesh of a face. This gave me new action that I hadn't figured on ahead of time. No one will stop reading at that point.

At the end of a chapter it's advisable to use the carryover of suspense. If you want to receive letters telling you that readers stayed up all hours reading one of your books — this is a good way to accomplish that. Most readers have the neat habit of setting a book down at the end of a chapter. So we prevent this in our own sneaky way.

Time is another important aid we can use in building suspense. If there is a threat that depends on time, the reader is held. Remember the movie, *High Noon*, and the inexorable hands of the clock? It isn't always possible to achieve that tight level of danger and suspense, but I find that when I can move my action along from day to day, this will give the reader a sense of being carried swiftly toward impending disaster. When there are lapses of time between scenes or chapters, there can be a slowing of interest. The necessities of plot govern this to some extent. When I was writing a Civil War novel, the events of history dictated the passage of time. When it's possible, the shorter time space lends its own momentum to what is happening.

A reader once wrote to me that my heroines were always changing their clothes and taking showers. That's what happens if you write from hour to hour. There are meals to eat, times to sleep — though no one wants too many details along the way. (I *have* cut down on the showers.) However you may use the time element, it needs to be considered in the building of suspense.

Another useful device to think about in the planning stage is to give every character a secret. As a writer you need to know about the hidden goals, the past guilts of every character. Such secrets can be used to make your story people behave in mysterious and suspense-building ways. As we think about and develop these secrets, the characters become more real to us, as writers, and thus to our readers. Conflict is likely to grow out of these concealed matters, and of course this is a main weapon in our suspense arsenal.

Car chases and fistfights aren't the most interesting type of conflict — Hollywood to the contrary. Holding a reader doesn't depend on violent action. It depends on *people action*. Is our sympathy engaged so we care enough about what is happening to the main character? Psychological conflict is the most interesting kind of all.

Two or more people sitting in a room talking can give us strong suspense, and be far more interesting than slamming into something physically. Conversation that builds and makes a reader curious is likely to provide surprise and hint at action to come. Suspense is not always achieved by jumping off a cliff. (Though that may be a culmination of all these other elements!)

Conflict grows out of well-conceived characters and strongly opposing goals. Which brings us back to that life-or-death problem our main character started out with. It's time to give that problem the ultimate test. What are the terrible penalties for failure? What are the satisfying rewards for success? If *happiness* is always the goal of the main character — to quote my favorite writing teacher, Dwight Swain — then let's build up the failures and rewards. It's a good idea to set these down on paper, and then consult what we've written from time to time — to keep us on the right track. The easiest thing the writer does is fool himself. So let's look at this in one of our more left brain states when we can be critical and objective.

Happiness may be the overall goal, but what is it *specifically*, that will make the main character happy? If you don't know, you are fooling yourself and your story will collapse.

Danger should be a main ingredient in a mystery novel. Sometimes it may be only a threat, but it must always be real. We dare not threaten the main character with something false that is supposed to scare the reader, but adds up to nothing. *It was all a mistake* is fatal to the writer. We try not to annoy.

Danger is of course easier to provide in an action novel when the main character is a man. The frailer sex (physically) had better not plunge into an obviously dangerous situation that she probably can't handle. Better not go walking down a dark alley alone when danger threatens. It's not very bright, and the reader will notice. Male characters too sometimes plunge into such situations, but they're more apt to get away with it.

There is a way around this for either sex. We must build up specific reasons why the main character is *forced* into danger. Because of these reasons (this and this and this — know what they are) the character *must* put himself/herself in jeopardy — and then has to be pretty ingenious to get out of it.

In a mystery novel, where there is certain to be a murderer and a death threat, how do we furnish an assault that won't be that overdone bop-on-the-head? Sometimes a threat can be as scary as an open attack. In my Charleston novel, my main character is backstage at night in a huge warehouse that has been turned into a theater. There are props all around, aisles of them, piled on shelves, tables, the floor. She stumbles up some unexpected steps when she hears someone creeping about, and falls, banging her head on an iron stove, knocking herself out. A self-imposed variety of the bop-on-the-head. When she comes to, she finds that some-one has placed an unusual weapon beside her—a long medieval halberd, with its axe head turned toward her. Its presence is creepy and threaten-ing. And perhaps more effective at this point than if it were used against her. It will turn up later!

The halberd is there because *I* found it in the cavernous backstage area of a theater in Charleston. It caught my imagination, and I took a flash picture to remind me. This is what can happen when you get out into the field and do active research. The more fresh impressions we put into our minds, the more we have to work with.

In the creation of suspense our choice of words is endlessly impor-tant. John Ciardi once wrote that words can have an emotional vote. So we must choose carefully. Not the trite and obvious that come so easily to mind, but words that will spring into life on their own and move the reader . . . to alarm, to astonishment, to delight, to terror. It's all done with the right words.

Verbs, of course, are important. Though I don't shun those adverbs and adjectives that we're sometimes told to avoid. Just don't overdo. I keep a book of synonyms at hand. *Roget's Thesaurus* has served me so well that I've worn out several copies. Endless pains may bring bigger checks in the long run.

Reveal new turns of the story and new information about the charac-ters gradually. Hold out. Build curiosity and milk it for a while. Tantalize, but not to so maddening a degree that the reader throws your book across the room. Pacing again! Feed in with partial answers, and then bring up new questions. The tempo should always rise and fall and rise again. The fall is that necessary rest period. Even slower scenes, however, can hold their own milder surprises and revelations.

As we near the climax, the threat of danger becomes more immi-nent, and we'd better handle this in an action scene. No more do we sit around a drawing room with our clever detective questioning and expos-ing suspects.

Emotions run high, possible avenues of escape are cut off—and there is no way out. How the solution is managed, and who is revealed as guilty, should surprise the reader. Most readers love to be fooled and are disappointed when they guess the ending. Satisfaction is important. An ending doesn't necessarily have to be happy to satisfy, but it has to be right.

At the end we *stop*. We stop because there is no more suspense, no more curiosity. We don't go on for pages boring the reader with explanations that should have been worked in earlier. This isn't easy. Perhaps we hold out the answer to one important question until the last paragraph — to pull the reader along. That easily read conclusion has often been rewritten a dozen times.

The greatest sigh of relief and satisfaction comes from the writer. All our travail, our brain-searching, our tired backs at the typewriter, have paid off and we've done it one more time.

I manage to feel quite giddy and free for about a week. Then I start searching so I can begin all over again. The writer is the one who never finishes the story.

CHAPTER 18

DEPICTION OF VIOLENCE

BILL GRANGER

The depiction of violence in novels is difficult for two reasons. The violence itself is both external and internal, objective and subjective; and the nature of the violent act described can impede the flow of narrative when the writer hopes that it will increase the flow.

External violence depicted in narration, oddly enough, is always in danger of becoming tedious.

How does a man shoot his victim? He pulls the trigger. The victim receives the bullet. The victim cries out or does not cry out. The victim falls or the victim stumbles and falls or the victim is thrown back by the force of the round. It is all anticlimax, in any case; the narrative tension has been used up in setting the final act of the scene. There are only so many ways of describing violent death, and they have all been done before.

Or, if the violence is short of dying, what makes it interesting as objective narration?

Like a barroom brawl in a John Ford western, smaller acts of violence — a sock to the jaw or a blackjack to the noggin — seem so predictable in fiction that the eye of the reader glazes over when he comes to it. This impedes the flow of the narrative, the second problem of depicting violence.

The wider world of fiction — movies, television scripts, et cetera — have inured us to shock at seeing violent acts. How much more difficult to portray violence in words? When cars crash into fireballs of death (something that can be seen nightly on the tube), the special effect is no longer special and has limited effect, except as punctuation at the end of the chase. And the punctuation is as muted as a period.

There are three good ways to describe external (or objective) violence in prose.

First, slow it down to the point of absurdity. Or, second, hide the act of violence in an empty bracket separating the before and after of the violence. Third, hide the horror of the act of violence (and all acts of violence rendered should be horrible) by deliberately underplaying the prose.

Here is an example of the first point.

"He fired. The round caught Henry below the right eye. A moment after the lead punctured the flesh and cracked the bone beneath the eye socket, Henry heard the sound of the gunshot and his eyes widened. He did not feel the impact of the bullet at all. The shooter stared at Henry's staring eyes while the round lost its velocity tearing up through the skull, through bone and brain, until it was stopped by the top of the skull. Henry was dead but his eyes remained wide open, still registering the sound of the gunshot in the closed, damp room."

Another example:

"The left front wheel of the Buick leapt the curb a moment before she felt the plastic steering wheel twist away from her grip. The wheel had developed a life apart from her intent. Two thousand pounds of Detroit machine hurtling sixty-one miles an hour down Garcia Road had entered a curve that could not be exited on mere wet pavement. The left front tire clawed at the sod and exploded over the neat row of hackenberry bushes and the rest of the automobile followed, the tires crying protest louder than Lydia's screams. A picket line of 200-year-old oak trees waited for the car just below the crest of the drive. The left front tire exploded when the rubber was pierced by a jagged stone but, by then, the rest of the automobile encasing Lydia Holman's body, was already being crushed by the unyielding trees."

In both illustrations, the moment of violence is just that but, because words dawdle at the pace of the reader, the writer has made them dawdle even more, to force the reader into the action. It is the writer's equivalent of Sam Peckinpah's celebrated slow-motion scenes of death without the worry of rendering the violence either beautiful or less horrifying (traps that Peckinpah let himself fall into).

Second point: Hide the external (objective) depiction in an empty bracket. The size of the bracket is determined by what went before and what comes after. The reader's eye is then forced to confront the empty bracket and *fill* it with his own invention of imagination which is generally more graphic than the writer's.

Example:

"Ninety-one minutes after takeoff from the wet, bumpy runway at Heathrow, George C. Scott stood in front of a giant American flag and pretended to be General George S. Patton addressing soldiers during World War II. Of the 197 persons in economy class, fifty-nine were watching Scott on the small movie screen at the front of their section of the cabin and twenty-three were asleep. Two of the four small, plastic washrooms were occupied by men who had whiled away the hour before boarding in one of the airport bars. Everyone in the overpacked economy class was uncomfortable but only two children, both too young to understand the silent endurance necessary for flight in the cheap seats, expressed their frustration by crying aloud. The Scott movie was also being shown in business and first-class sections where drinks were served in real glasses. Scott said all Americans love to fight. A man who sat in the aisle seat in first class opened his Zenith laptop and turned it on. The pilot told the navigator the one he had heard that morning over coffee in the Hilton, not usually a time of day for good or even funny jokes.

"A moment later, the radar screen of Air France 121 trailing eleven miles behind made the green dot that was Flight 901 disappear. The Parisian navigator looked at the screen, blinked, turned a knob, and said something to the captain. Both men looked out the windshield. The day was full of sun and all the clouds were beneath their wings. Between the clouds were patches of the blue Atlantic. They were four minutes south and east of Iceland. 'Mon Dieu,' the captain said. He blessed himself; he was from Marseilles. He saw nothing in front of him but the long, clear day."

Another example:

" 'Please take your wallet back.' The smiling man extended the wallet. He had taken only the money. James did not move.

" 'Please.' The smiling man held the wallet out only a few inches from his chest. James had to take a step nearer to grasp the wallet he had surrendered a moment before. The man made his smile wider and more sincere. There was no one else on the subway platform, as though the throbbing night city above had suddenly forgotten all the trains and stations and miles of track below. James touched the wallet. Then he saw the knife. The knife had been there all along but James only now saw it.

"The first policeman knelt on one knee on the subway station platform. He was careful not to kneel too close to the body. The policeman said, 'He must have been very strong.'

"The second policeman said, 'You can't just cut like that. He cut all the way across. Nobody cuts like that.'

"The kneeling policeman said, 'His wallet. He's got his wallet in his hand. Why didn't he just give him the wallet? Money isn't that important. Christ, he must have been strong, whoever did it, to cut like that. It must have been a helluva big knife to get that much cut in it.' "

Third point: Underplay the prose. This is still most effective in police procedurals but it can be used in all categories of the thriller. The narration of violence does not have to be cop-like or even acquire a Joe Friday monotone. Understatement is the key to making this approach to depiction of violence successful.

Here is a rape scene. The rape scene is graphic but it has two inherent problems common to all depictions of violent sexual assault. It must not be prurient. It must not excite any feeling except horror. On the other hand, if it is too graphic, it will turn off readers and destroy the narrative flow, at least temporarily. The third approach to depiction of objective violence is the most useful (although the second approach — the empty bracket — might be preferred by some writers. The first approach — slowing the action — cannot be used with falling into the traps set by the inherent problems described above.)

"The two men followed her to the C level of the empty garage. She dropped her keys and bent to pick them up. Her hands were shaking. Her heels clicked loudly on the cement and she fumbled with the keys in her hand, trying to find the door lock key. They were so close to her now that she couldn't turn around. Maybe they were kids, just kids. The first man stood behind her and the second man went to the driver's side door. He looked at her. She did not look at him. She put the wrong key in the lock.

"He hit her very hard across the face and she screamed. He hit her again and told her not to scream. She saw the knife. She started to speak and he hit her again.

"The second man laughed and grabbed her shoulders. The first man pushed her down on the cement. She turned her head and saw an oil spot on the floor of the garage beneath her car's motor. She stared at the spot. Her ears rang from the force of the blows. The first one forced her legs apart and then it began. She bit her lip and closed her eyes. When she opened them again, she had drawn blood from her lip and the oil spot was on the cement below the motor housing. Maybe there was something wrong with the car. She smelled them but she couldn't look at them.

"She felt one and then the other and then the second one hit her again and she began to cry. The first one said something to her and then hit her again and she kept crying. The second one said to stop hitting her. The first one stood over her and said they ought to kill her. She heard that above the ringing in her ears. The second one said he was going to split. The first one lifted her purse and opened it. The second one said he was going to split. She said nothing. She turned her face toward the car and saw the oil spot on the cement just as it had been a moment before. She was crying but she didn't hear it. She didn't hear them running down the ramps to the street. She just saw the oil on the floor of the garage and had to keep staring at it."

There is a touch of Hemingway in using the third method in depiction of objective violence but that is simply because Hemingway did it better than anyone else. Simple sentences or long sentences connected by strings of "ands" and "buts" and deliberately stripped of descriptive language are very powerful instruments in writing about violent acts. The understated approach borrows a little from the "empty bracket" way by bringing up irrelevancies and giving them prominence — the victim of the rape stares at the oil spot on the garage floor. There is no hidden meaning in that focus but it carries weight simply because the writer (and reader) are imagining the action so bleakly described.

Incidentally, there is no point in slowing down detail (or stripping detail of description) to the point of giving an anatomy lesson. A graphic rape description would be unbearable (note Garp's first chapter of a proposed novel in John Irving's book; it is so long, horrible, prurient and unbearable that the editor can't believe it's only the first chapter). Anatomy lessons almost always deaden narration, if not at the time then in everything that follows.

Back to the third method of depicting objective violence. Here is another example, about death on an army firing range.

"The instructor in the tower was shouting into the microphone. While he shouted the instruction to lock and load one clip into the rifles, Tommy Leary shoved the butt on the M1 into the hollow between his shoulder and his rib cage. He sighted the rifle and saw a deer on the slope beyond the paper targets. The deer stared at the tower, at the row of soldiers sprawled in the prone firing position on the red clay. Tommy Leary dug his elbows into the ground and he was staring at the white-tailed deer.

"The word 'Fire' was followed by a chorus of shots. Some of the men fired very quickly and some of them fired in careful steps, first one and then another and then another, the shells flipping up from the firing chamber and to the right, out of the way. The left-handed soldiers had a problem because the rifle was designed for right-handers and the spent shells flipped across their line of vision. Tommy was right-handed. He fired twice and then he shifted a little and brought the rifle around and Sergeant Mackelson was at the end of the sights, fixed vertically on the front hair and horizontally on the rear sight, about halfway up his belly. Tommy Leary fired twice and Sergeant Mackelson leaped out of sight and fell down the firing line ridge. Tommy Leary turned the rifle back to the target line by rolling on the flat of his belly and the deer stood still on the slope the way deer do and Tommy lobbed a shot over the target line towards the slope. The deer didn't move. He was too far away. 'Cease firing, cease firing' the instructor was screaming into the microphone but some were still popping shots at the targets. Tommy released his finger from the trigger. He had two rounds in the clip left."

Depiction of violence subjectively is, on the face of it, easier. But it is actually much more difficult if done well enough not to interrupt the narration. Take the rape scene above. It can be rendered subjectively but how do you do it without falling into clichés or falling into the trap of prurience?

Subjective depiction, to be successful, uses a small brush on a big canvas that is never filled. It is concerned with detail and the shock that external violence has on the subject. For example, a person who has been shot or stabbed rarely sees the objective horror of what was done to him (her). I once talked—with detectives—to a man who had been stabbed twenty-three times in the chest by his girlfriend. He was hooked to syrup and plasma, he had been slightly doped, and some of his wounds were superficial but . . . twenty-three times is twenty-three times. The cops wanted to know who did it (the girlfriend part came later) and the guy kept saying he had cut himself in the bathroom shaving. He just couldn't believe he had been stabbed twenty-three times.

Gunshot victims say the same sort of thing in real life. Days or weeks later, they reconstruct the narrative of the violence done them from an external (objective) point of view because that is the context everyone else has dealt with and they have learned it the way Americans learn

French in Paris — in self-defense in the war of communications.

In short, the act of violence is usually a period in punctuation whereas everything leading up to it is exclamation.

This example is from one of my novels. I've edited it a bit using the ellipsis method to get to the core of the illustration:

"She stepped out into the bright October light. The sunlight was fragmented against the golden maples behind the apartment complex . . . Rita Macklin stepped onto the new gravel on the lot, stopped, smiled at the sky and trees. The bad thoughts about Devereaux had left her; she would be all right the rest of the day . . . She fumbled for her car keys in her purse and pulled them out. The car was a five-year-old Ford Escort, a minimal sort of car . . . (A long passage describes the car, her life-style, her job, her attitude, a sort of going-nowhere stream of consciousness, and then) . . . She had her keys in hand as she reached the car. In the next moment, she was on the ground. She had fallen, she thought. She felt a dull sickness in her stomach and wondered if she had broken the heel of her right shoe. The shoes cost $125, which was obscene, but she had loved them when she saw them in the store on L Street. She thought her skirt would be soiled by the gravel and the dirt in the parking lot. A stupid fall and she had ruined her clothes and would have to change and miss the next flight . . ."

Rita has been shot but not until a neighbor tells her she has been shot do we know it, though obviously something has happened. The point is, Rita — like most of us — is finding it hard to connect her world of interior monologue with what is happening around her, or, in this case, to her.

The subjective side of depiction of violence is most useful when it underscores the violence by ironic understatement or misstatement. Rita thinks about her shoes, her clothes, the reason she owns a car, thinks about falling down and missing her plane . . . all of it faintly comic in its triviality weighed against the gravity of the violence done her. Sympathy for the victim can be evoked subjectively very well by using a sort of stream-of-consciousness narrative that runs parallel and counter to the objective action.

Let's say a man is shoved in front of an El train in Chicago. Try it this way:

"The train suddenly rounded the curve between the apartment buildings and the crowd along the narrow wooden platform stirred. Steve took a half step closer to the edge, looked at the train, looked down at the tracks above the street, looked at his shoes, clenched the Tribune in his hand, looked up again. The train rattled the wood-and-steel structure of the elevated line.

"The tracks were wet from the morning rain and the third rail threw up showers of sparks. It was beautiful and dramatic and Steve smiled because it reminded him of the old man on the day the old man had taken him for his first El ride.

"Steve's father had told him about the third rail, had told him that he would be dead in an instant if he ever touched the third rail. He had been so solemn that little Steve almost did not believe him until he saw the sparks showered up by a passing train.

"And, in that moment, he fell.

"He was on his knees on the tracks, the street was visible below between the ties, he could see the top of a green-and-white bus.

"Steve blinked at the train screeching fifty feet in front of him. He stared at the double headlights. It was wasteful to have them on in broad daylight, it was broad daylight, he was going to QEM Productions and the El would be quicker and cheaper and he saw his father telling him about the third rail and the possibilities of violent death on the El, about a man who had fallen from a train, about a train that had once fallen from the tracks in the Loop . . . his sweet, cautionary father and all the sweet times of his life and the sweet, sweet smell of early summer when the grass was first cut and the third rail, he must never touch the third rail, but his father was not always right about everything and Steve had to grow up and get a job and live alone and take the El to QEM and the noise of the train screeching was even louder than his scream."

(I apologize to every English teacher for that sentence but I liked it anyway.)

I like the disjointed narrative in subjective depiction because it resembles, for me, the random, rimfire shooting of dreams during REM sleep and the victim feeling you have when you are caught in a dream and cannot move or speak or act.

"He knew it was dangerous. He was frightened all the time, even when he slept and he was safe and there were locks on the door. He thought about Sheila in that bed that one time when they had locked all the locks and taken off each other's clothes and not said a word as they got on the bed. On the bed. And then the shooting stopped. Just like that. He blinked to hear it better but it was definitely quiet, very quiet, too quiet, quiet like the grave the way Healy would say. Sheila never said a word. He was on his knees and that meant he had been shot. He didn't feel pain and he knew that they did not always feel pain at first, that some of them in the hospital said they never felt pain until the surgery was over; in any case, he had been shot. Sheila opened her legs and smiled and he slid onto her lap and into her.

"There was absolutely no pain at all and Sheila never said a word, it was so quiet, just like now, the silence had a sound to it because it was so intense and it would be all right to lie down now, Sheila said it was all right, and the ground was as soft and yielding as a bed, as laying down in Sheila's lap in the dark silence of the locked room."

Finally, the question to be asked of violence in narration is what purpose it will serve. Violence in itself is a willing character and this sometimes fools a writer into thinking the amiable clod can do everything he claims. Violence as character is deceitful to the writer and can lull the writer to laziness. If the narration is slowing down, violence suggests a shot of itself will pep the thing up; in most cases, it merely points out how weak the narration has been up to then and how weak it is following the pep pill of violence.

The world is violent, so violent that we become inured to depictions of violence. The coin of violence has been debased by screenwriters who patch up leaky TV and movie scripts with violence that is merely routinely spectacular. The clichés of TV and movies make it much harder for novelists and short story writers to convey the suspense and horror of violence.

The writer should remember the old newspaperism that violence only counts when it touches home. A ferry overturning in India in which a thousand died does not move the heart as surely as the death of a boy trapped in a well in Texas or the murder of a grandmother down the block. Tragedy is personal, and violence, tragedy's sister, best serves the writer when it is personal. The best way to make it personal is not to stage John Ford fights in saloons but to bring the haunting finality of tragedy to it.

If you do not believe in the violence—if you are not affected by it at the moment you write it down—then you are a hack and do a disservice to your reader or are really engaging in comedy. Life is not all Ingmar Bergman but it isn't all Roger Rabbit either; the bigger the paintbrush of violence, the less real it is. Depictions of violence are miniatures.

CHAPTER 19

CLUES, RED HERRINGS AND OTHER PLOT DEVICES

P.M. CARLSON

"But I want *you* to be the victim. And the person who kills you can be Deirdre Henderson. The repressed plain girl whom nobody notices."

"There you are, Ariadne," said Robin. "The whole plot of your next novel presented to you. All you'll have to do is work in a few false clues, and — of course — do the actual writing."

— Agatha Christie
Mrs. McGinty's Dead

"All you'll have to do is work in a few false clues. . . . " Yeah, sure. Anyone who's ever tried to plot a mystery knows that Robin's careless words to Ariadne Oliver gloss over one of the most difficult and most important aspects of plotting.

My own books generally start with a complicated cluster of an un-usual motive or an unusual murder method with a setting that I find interesting and a character or two whose problems I want to explore. Even at this primitive stage it's almost impossible to answer the cocktail-party question, "Where do you get your ideas?" because a lot of sources have already fed into the cluster. But once this cluster of "ideas" has jelled into the basic triangle of victim, murderer and detective, the hard work of plotting begins.

A logical story of the murder must be laid out early, of course, even though it will be revealed in a less logical order and won't be seen in full until the end of the book. Signs of this logical story must be thought-out carefully for the detective (and reader) to discover as the story progresses. At this early stage I try not to tie things down too much. My notes are full of question marks—maybe this, maybe that—but it's important to me to get a rough sketch of the true direction to be tracked. I'll be subjecting my detective to plenty of distractions and agonies, but this is the trail my hunter must ultimately follow. As Watson writes of Sherlock Holmes in "The Boscombe Valley Mystery,"

> Men who had only known the quiet thinker and logician of Baker Street would have failed to recognize him. His face flushed and darkened. His brows were drawn into two hard black lines, while his eyes shone out from beneath them with a steely glitter. His face was bent downward, his shoul-ders bowed, his lips compressed, and his veins stood out like whipcord in his long, sinewy neck. His nostrils seemed to dilate with a purely animal lust for the chase, and his mind was so absolutely concentrated upon the matter be-fore him that a question or remark fell unheeded upon his ears, or, at the most, only provoked a quick, impatient snarl in reply.

The metaphor of detective as hunting dog hot on the scent has been with us for a long time. And it's useful to remind myself that readers too are hot on the scent, a whole pack of eager hounds chasing after my foxy murderer. Some readers are wily old hunters who know all the tricks and keep up with the detective or even surge ahead for a few pages; others are mere pups, easily distracted by the scenery. All of them enjoy the chase, and all of them deserve a good hunt.

Enter the red herring.

The original red herring was a smoked herring, actually more brown-ish than red, with a powerful scent very attractive to hunting dogs. It was dragged across the true trail to try to distract the hounds from their real objective. In a detective story, the distraction must be similarly powerful.

So once I've outlined the basic story of the victim and the murderer, together with the unusual motive or unusual murder method that links them, I go back to the victim and think about him or her. Who else might want this person murdered, and why? Several more stories have to be outlined about people who have good reasons to desire the victim dead, and who have the means and opportunity to kill the victim. At this point I often start grumbling that a mystery writer's lot is not a happy one, and why didn't I decide to write the kind of novels where one plot is enough?

But I plug away, thinking up more stories, still with lots of maybes and question marks. The task is harder because, like the original red herrings dragged across a trail, these extra stories should cross the true murder story from time to time.

For example, suppose we want to write a story that includes a gourmet cook — we'll call him Dan. In a gourmet shop window we notice a handsome marble rolling pin, used for French pastries. We, of course, are not attracted by the thought of crisp, airy Napoleons and éclairs. Well, okay, we *are* attracted by the thought, but even more by the thought that this is the ideal blunt instrument for the plot we're hatching. It's unusual and distinctive, and heavy. It can definitely be a clue on our true trail. So, first, we make sure that our murderer is able to lay hands on our (now fictional) marble rolling pin in time to do the murder. If Dan the gourmet cook is the murderer, we may decide that this distinctive weapon will be the decisive clue — he is the *only* person who has access to it. In this case, we'll probably want to have it disappear from the scene of the crime, hidden somehow by clever Dan. Throughout the book, then, the detective, the police, and (we hope) the readers will be wondering about the weapon used.

Now, how do we confuse the trail? One way is to give our red herring characters access to similar objects. Perhaps one character is remodeling a room, and has a tool chest with a variety of hammers and mallets. Another character may be a golfer with a handsome trophy that has a cylindrical, heavy pedestal base. But only our detective notices that Dan the gourmet cook has recently rearranged his collection of expensive kitchen implements to mask the absence of a rolling pin.

On the other hand, maybe we don't want Dan to be the murderer. We can still provide false weapons to various characters as above. Or we may want the true weapon to be identified early in the story. Now the game is to provide access to the weapon for several red herring characters. Dan owns the rolling pin. Let's suppose he keeps it in his kitchen, in full view. In that case his family and guests have access to it. When? We can narrow down the time to the few minutes of a visit, or expand it. For example, Agatha Christie has a crucial weapon turn up in Suspect A's house — but it turns out that it was purchased at a church sale, donated by Suspect B, and no one can remember if it was the sale preceding the murder or the sale following the murder. Furthermore, Suspect A's house is a boardinghouse and is never kept locked, so the entire village may have had access to the weapon at the time of the murder.

We can also narrow the field of suspects to a few who had opportunity to steal the weapon, and then widen the field later in the book. For example, let's suppose that the owner of the lethal marble rolling pin, Dan, cooks a gourmet meal for several suspects — Ann, Jan and Fran. Naturally the rolling pin disappears at this time. We know that Stan and Nan have never been near Dan's kitchen. Now, after much detective work, we learn that in fact Ann is the one who took the rolling pin from Dan's kitchen, but she claims she lost it. Things are looking bad for her, when — aha! — our detective remembers that Stan or Nan could have stolen it from Ann's bag when they met her on the way home from Dan's.

A truly foxy murderer will probably create false clues too. In that classic maze of false trails, *The Five Red Herrings* by Dorothy L. Sayers, the murderer provides himself with an alibi using a complicated bucketful of false clues including meals, bicycles, painting techniques, clothing, and most notoriously, train schedules. Luckily for Lord Peter Wimsey, the murderer makes one small mistake in his haste, so that after the lies are stripped away from the stories of the five red herring characters, Wimsey is able to reconstruct the crime and cover-up in almost every elaborate detail. When I'm sketching in my alternate stories, I often find it useful to lay out a big chart showing each character's activities at the crucial times in the narrative. It boggles the mind to think of what Sayers's chart for *The Five Red Herrings* must have looked like.

One device Sayers did not use in that book was the frame — the situation in which the true target is not the murder victim, but someone who will be falsely accused of the crime. In a case like this, the detective's usual starting point — the victim's life — may turn out to be largely red herrings, and there will be many circumstantial clues pointing to the wrong person. It is not until the investigation turns to the accused person's life that progress is made.

Since my books are often fair play whodunits, I've been concentrating so far on the kinds of plots that are used in such books. In the classic fair play whodunit formula, there are perhaps half a dozen suspects, and the clues and false clues point first at one, then at another, in an even-handed way.

Clues and red herrings may be handled a little differently in the classic quest formula, typical of many private eye books. While the same kinds of misdirections that I've been talking about will work, and many private eye plots involve wondering which of several suspects may be behind the gore, there is often a shift of emphasis. The trail may occupy a smaller proportion of the book, for many reasons. In a country house whodunit, for example, the world that led up to the murder is given from the beginning. But a private eye in Sara Paretsky's Chicago, or Robert Crais's Los Angeles, or Sue Grafton's Santa Teresa lives among wide-open possibilities. The first task is often to discover which of the many worlds inhabited by the victim is the one that got him into trouble. Did he do drugs? Did he embezzle from his firm? Did he have gambling debts? Did he cheat on his wife? While all of these questions may eventually arise in the closed world of classic puzzle mysteries, a private eye often has to do extensive preliminary work before the appropriate set of suspects even appears. To use the foxhound analogy, the detective has to hunt through several fields before he even picks up the scent of the true fox.

A quest plot may also give more emphasis to the final overcoming of the quarry. Once the fox is found and cornered, there's a bigger fight — as though the fox turned out to be a wolf pack that outnumbered our lonely private eye. Several chapters may be devoted to the excitement and danger as the detective uses all her intelligence and physical ability to plan and carry out the defeat of the awesome adversary.

Because the private eye may need more chapters to find the correct trail, and more chapters to overcome the villain, the actual trail-following aspect of a quest plot may end up being considerably shorter and more straightforward than that of a puzzle plot. Weapons tend to be guns rather than unknown blunt instruments that turn out to be gourmet kitchen implements. Progress along the true trail may be blocked by simpler means than the elaborate counterplots of Wimsey's or Miss Marple's adversaries: a bureaucrat refuses to release needed information, or the villain's henchmen beat up the detective and make off with the only known clue, or the client gets cold feet and tries to stop the private eye from proceeding.

My favorite obstacles are those that grow from character. My detective Maggie Ryan is a loving parent and sometimes has difficulty believing evil can be done by others who love children. Keith Peterson's tough investigative reporter in *The Trapdoor* is haunted by his only daughter's suicide, and must courageously overcome enormous psychological obstacles to discover the truth about a rash of teen suicides. Even Lord Peter must struggle occasionally to go on with the hunt because he is shattered at the thought of the punishment the murderer must undergo. There are many possible plot devices like these to intensify the interest of the story even while blocking progress toward the solution.

"All you'll have to do is work in a few false clues." It's a long and sometimes painful stage of mystery writing — but as things fall into place, as our stories full of question marks and maybes are braided into a fine wriggly plot, it's a matter of fun and even pride. And when you're done? Well, as Agatha Christie's character says so offhandedly, we must, of course, "do the actual writing." But someone else can tell you about *that* little difficulty.

CHAPTER 20

THE BOOK STOPS HERE

LAWRENCE BLOCK

It's the most mysterious thing. You're working on a book, plugging away at it like The Little Engine That Could, turning out a page a day or five pages a day or ten pages a day, watching those finished pages pile up and beginning to see the light at the end of the tunnel. You don't want to get too cocky, don't want to get the Big Editor in the Sky mad at you, but, by George, it certainly looks as though you've breezed past the halfway mark and are closing fast on the three-quarter pole. All you have to do is keep showing up for work every day, keep putting your behind on the chair and your fingers on the keys, and it's just a matter of time, and not too much time at that, before the book will be finished.

Oh, you may still have work to do. Some light revision at the very least. Maybe a formal second draft. No matter, that's the easy part, what the military would call a mopping-up operation. When your first draft is done your book is written, and you can jump up and down and call people and celebrate and even take that shower you've been promising yourself for so long. And the first draft's almost done, it'll be done any minute, all you have to do is keep at it and—

And, all of a sudden, kablooey.

You're stuck. The book's going nowhere. It's dead in the water, finished, kaput.

Now what?

The conventional wisdom holds that what I've just described is a disaster, and it's not terrribly hard to guess how it became the conventional wisdom. The conventional wisdom goes further to suggest that the thing to do when a book gets stuck is to lower your metaphorical head and charge forward. (It helps, I suppose, if you're wearing a metaphorical helmet.) By pushing on, by damning the torpedos and going full speed ahead, you can go right through whatever's impeding you and get the book finished as planned. You can turn a deaf ear to the voice that keeps telling you there's something wrong. You can brush all those doubts and anxieties right out of your mind. Casting them as the road and yourself as the chicken, you can Get To The Other Side.

Well, sure. And sometimes that's exactly what you ought to do.

And sometimes it's not.

When a book grinds to a halt, it may have done so for a reason. To avoid looking for the reason is a little like overlooking the trouble lights on a car's dashboard. You can run the car when those lights go on, and you can even do as the previous owner of my car seems to have done, disconnecting a wire so that the lights won't bug you like some sort of mechanical conscience. Maybe you'll wind up all right, but there's a good chance that sooner or later they'll come for you with a tow truck.

A couple of examples. Several years ago, I was writing the fifth volume in a series of mysteries about Bernie Rhodenbarr, a burglar and bookseller by profession, a solver of homicides by circumstance. I was 180 pages into what looked likely to be a 300-page manuscript, when Something Went Wrong. I spent a day staring at the typewriter without getting anything done. I took a day off, and another day off. By the end of the week I realized that I was in trouble. I didn't know what was wrong, but I knew something was wrong.

Now I could have barreled through it and forced the book over the finish line. I knew who the killer was, and how and why the crime had taken place. I had not painted myself into any impossible plot corners. But there was something wrong, and I couldn't see how to fix it, not least of all because I wasn't altogether sure what it was.

I still don't know exactly what was wrong. I think there was something gone off-stroke in the book's timing. I can't tell you how or why I screwed it up in the first place, or just what enabled me to fix it. I know what happened—I moped around for a few weeks, during which time I despaired that the book would join the great body of manuscripts I've abandoned forever over the years. While this was happening, I suspect a portion of my unconscious mind was playing with the problem and looking for a solution. One evening I had a long conversation about the book with a friend of mine. I don't recall what either of us said, or that a specific solution came out of our conversation, but I walked away from it somehow knowing how to proceed. I started the book over from the beginning, using most of the scenes I had written but fitting them together somewhat differently, and running the whole thing through the typewriter again. This time, everything worked. I finished the book without a snag, and I think it's the best one in the series.

I probably could have finished the book by just staying with it and forcing myself to write. And it probably would have been publishable. But I'm sure it was better for my having had trouble with it, and for having surrendered to the trouble instead of trying to ride roughshod over it.

More recently, six months ago I settled in and went to work on a new Matthew Scudder novel. I'd spent half a year thinking about the book and felt ready to write it. I had no trouble getting started, worked at a fast clip, and had 200 pages written in a couple of weeks. The writing went well, and I was pleased with the scenes and characters that I had developed.

But, by the time I was a little ways past the halfway mark, I realized that I'd managed a kind of reverse synergy—i.e., the whole of what I'd written was rather less than the sum of its parts. The book was taking too long to get going, and it was wandering off in far too many directions. Some of my best scenes and characters were just marking time, doing nothing to advance the plot. And the plot itself was unwieldy and unworkable. I was going to have to start over. The story I wanted to write was in there somewhere, and I had a feeling I could find it, but all of that would have to wait. I needed time away from the book, and eventually I would have to scrap 90 percent of what I'd written and start over from the beginning.

This didn't mean what I'd written was a waste of time; it was all part of the process, and I evidently had to go through it in order to find the story I'll eventually write. (At least I hope I'll eventually write it, if all of this is to have a happy ending.)

Again, I could have forced myself to keep writing, could have overruled my own doubts and anxieties. And I could have finished the book that way. It wouldn't have been very good, and I'm not sure it would have been publishable, but you never know what is or isn't publishable these days. It certainly wouldn't have emerged as a book I would have been pleased with.

The implication would seem to be clear: If you get stuck on a book, there must be something wrong with it. Set it aside or fix it.

But I could furnish other examples that would seem to prove the opposite. I have had books stall in much the same fashion, have pushed on and seen them through to completion, and have had them turn out just fine. Some years ago, when I was writing a series of paperback suspense novels about a sort of freelance spy named Evan Tanner, I noticed that I always seemed to hit a bad patch somewhere around page 125. (The Tanner books ran around 200 pages in manuscript.) I always stayed with what I was writing, and the books always worked out all right, and when I read them over afterward there was no evident sag or quagmire around page 125.

I suspect what happened was that I tended to have a sort of failure of confidence at around that point. Once I got a chapter or so further along in the work, my confidence returned of its own accord and I felt capable of completing the work. I don't know the source of this, but I have a hunch it had more to do with me than with the work. Years later, during my career as the world's slowest but most determined long-distance runner, I experienced a similar sinking feeling at about the same stage — say, six miles into a ten-mile race. There would be a point at which I felt I really ought to drop out of the race, that to go further would only result in injury, that I couldn't possibly go the distance. I never did quit a race short of the finish (although there were times I probably should have) and once I got a kilometer or so past that crisis point I always knew I would make it. The two processes are vastly different, and none of my runs were the athletic equivalent of publishable, but I don't think it was coincidental that I tended to feel on the verge of failure at the same point in books as in races.

On the other hand, maybe I only noticed crises of this sort when they came at that particular stage, a little past the halfway mark. Maybe I had comparable crises, comparable failures of nerve, at other points along the way — but I didn't recognize them for what they were.

I was packing my office not long ago and I came across two thirty-page chunks of manuscript, one written two years ago, the other a little older. Each was the opening of a novel about Bernie Rhodenbarr, and each had been forever abandoned around the thirtieth page. I had stopped working on them because they just plain weren't working. The writing felt labored, the dialogue seemed flat, and I wisely stopped work on them and said the hell with it.

Well, I read both of those chunks of manuscript, and I was amazed. I don't have a clue what I thought was wrong with them at the time I stopped work on them. My writing seemed as spritely as it ever gets, my dialogue was as crisp and lively as I could have wanted it, and all either manuscript lacked to be perfectly publishable was another 270 pages in the same vein. Looking back, it strikes me as highly probable that I would have been incapable of producing those 270 pages back then, and an unconscious recognition of this fact soured me on what I was writing. Not really wanting to go on, I decided that the grapes I'd already reached were sour.

The point, though, is that in neither case did I feel I'd hit a snag. Instead I just figured I'd had a false start, and one that only represented the work of a couple of days. I have tossed off and subsequently tossed out a chapter of a book or a few pages of a short story on more occasions than I can remember, and so have most writers I know, and so what? You can't expect the world to salute every time you run one up the flagpole. Often the only way to find out if something is going to work is to try writing it, and to drop it if it fizzles out.

You can avoid this sort of false start if you never write anything without having it clear in your mind, but you might miss out on a lot of stories that way. Donald Westlake wrote an opening chapter once because he had this image of a guy crossing the George Washington Bridge on foot. He didn't know who the guy was or why he was walking across the bridge, but decided that he (like the guy) could cross that bridge when he came to it. The book turned out to be *The Hunter*, the first of sixteen books (under the pseudonym of "Richard Stark") about a professional criminal named Parker, who the guy on the bridge turned out to be.

And if it hadn't worked out that way, if Parker, upon crossing the bridge, had turned into a drugstore instead of turning into a terrific series character, well, so what? Don would have wasted a day's work, and we all do that often enough, don't we?

You might think that outlining could make a difference, especially in avoiding snags late in the game, where the book is two-thirds written and you can't think of a thing to have happen on the next page. If you've got a detailed outline, all of those problems are presumably worked out in advance. The book can't hit a real snag because you always know what's going to happen next.

Sure you do.

Although I haven't outlined anything in quite a few years now, I used outlines on many occasions over the years, some of them sketchy, others more elaborate. And it's unarguably true that a writer working from an outline always knows what he originally intended to have happen next.

But there's no guarantee it'll work. Sometimes the novel proves to have a will of its own and veers away from the outline. This isn't necessarily a bad thing, but it does mean that you have nothing but your imagination and your vocabulary to help you figure out what happens next.

And, even when the plot hews close to what you've outlined, there's no guarantee that what worked in outline will work in manuscript. Sometimes, indeed, a novel will stall out around the two-thirds or the three-quarters mark because the outlined plot just isn't working and the writer's unable to loosen up and make the necessary departures from it.

So what's the answer?

Beats me. Every book is a case unto itself, and every time we sit down to write one we take a plunge into uncharted waters. It is a hazardous business, this novel-writing dodge, and it doesn't cease to be so after long years in the game. Novelists who have been at it since Everest was a molehill still find themselves leaving a book unfinished, or finishing an unpublishable one. (Sometimes a good writer gets away with a bad book, and publishes it, and sometimes it sells as well as his good books, but only one's accountant is gladdened when that sort of thing happens. The object is not to sneak by with a bad book, it's to write a good one.)

So, when a book hits a snag and the sun goes out and the moon turns black, do you:

1. Keep right on going and finish it? or

2. Figure out where you went wrong and make it right? or

3. Decide that it doesn't say Purina, and bury it in the yard?

The answer, I guess, is:

4. Any or all of the above, depending.

All you have to do is figure out which, and you have to figure it out anew each time it happens.

Look, I never said this was going to be easy.

CHAPTER 21

IN THE
BEGINNING
IS THE
END

JOHN LUTZ

O f course!" you think, as you read the last paragraph or sentence of a successful mystery short story or novel, "this is how everything *had* to turn out." The ending does more than simply surprise you. It seems not only possible but plausible. That's because the writer knew from the beginning where the story was going.

Writing is an extremely individualistic endeavor, so none of the rules apply to everyone. There are a few writers who sit down and begin a tale without a scintilla of an idea as to where it's headed. Most of these writers never sell anything. Some do, and some of them are superb writers, but they're members of a small minority among the professionals I know. If you're sure you're one of these rare and wondrous creatures, move on to another section of this book, and good luck.

Still with me? Good. I think the odds are better for our kind of writer. Beginning a work of fiction without having at least some idea as to the ending is something like jumping into your car and driving away without any idea as to your destination. It's true you might arrive someplace interesting, but you're sure to meander getting there and spend time driving through plenty of not-so-interesting places. And meandering, digressing, is fatal to good fiction.

As in taking a trip by car, you need to know your destination before you set out. And, in fiction, the trip should be at least half the fun. When you and the reader reach the destination at the end of the story or novel, the reader will remember how the two of you got there, and the more direct, memorable and plausible the journey, the better. The techniques of foreshadowing and the planting of clues are invaluable in creating the above qualities, in preparing the reader for the destination only you know about.

To write good mystery fiction, you should know the difference between these two techniques, keeping in mind that while they are, by definition, different elements of fiction, the distinction isn't always clear and there is some overlapping.

The planting of clues is exactly what the term implies. Let's say you're writing a short story wherein Colonel Mustard has been found dead in his study, a knife wound in his chest but no weapon in the room. All doors and windows have been locked from the inside, and there are no hiding places or hidden passages. There are no footprints in the freshly fallen snow beneath the windows or surrounding the house, and all of the houses's occupants have ironclad alibis.

Now, let me explain the missing weapon. Fortunately we're not really writing this story, because I have no idea how to explain the rest of the circumstances, as I had no idea how to explain them when I sat down and wrote this. Do you have any ideas? See what I mean about how this can get you into trouble?

The missing knife, as many of you have no doubt guessed, was fashioned from a blade of ice which, after being wielded as the murder weapon, melted. Now, if you were to create a blood-tinted puddle near the body, which your detective will later determine is the melted weapon, you would be creating a clue. The reader, as well as your detective, would know about this puddle and have a chance — a slim one, if you've written this correctly — to figure out what it means. At tale's end, the detective could point out the presence of this puddle to some of the other characters, as well as to the reader, as evidence leading to his or her conclusion about the method of murder. And of course method often leads to opportunity, motive and suspect. So, a clue.

If you were to make the colonel's study uncommonly warm, mention that the eventually-to-be-revealed murderer was seen getting a midnight snack from the freezer, drop the fact that one of the suspects was earlier leaning out a window (above which, icicles hang) and wearing gloves (needed to wield the icy dagger), you have foreshadowed.

The puddle next to the corpse was certainly made by something, is tangible and remarkable, and *must* mean something, even if it isn't relevant to the murder. It requires an explanation, if the writer is to keep faith with the reader. But the above mentioned circumstances don't necessarily mean anything other than what they appear to mean. It might well be that the murder simply occurred on a relatively warm day, that the suspect raiding the refrigerator merely had an attack of the munchies, and certainly there's nothing unusual about wearing gloves in winter; the writer might well be remiss in *not* mentioning gloves in a description of the suspect's outdoor attire. Yet because these elements are part of the story, when the reader gets to the final paragraphs, he or she will find the explanation of the frozen weapon plausible. Committing murder this way is certainly possible, and the puddle as *clue* will lend the impression that if the reader had been just a bit sharper in regard to that in particular, he or she might have figured out this entire nasty business a few steps ahead of your detective.

Notice I said "impression." You shouldn't actually give your readers a chance to be a jump ahead of your detective, or those successful in doing so will be disappointed at not being fooled, and reviewers who manage to figure things out prematurely will impolitely suggest that maybe you should give up writing and sell insurance, or perhaps surrender your firstborn and slit your wrists for wasting their time and straining their eyes.

Okay we've taken care of both possibility and plausibility: The puddle as clue, since its presence from the beginning suggests some explanation is needed, and that explanation falls solidly within the realm of possibility. And as foreshadowing we've provided weather, snack and gloves; they don't necessarily mean anything unusual, but at the end of the story they do add up to plausibility.

Clues provide the eventual explanation of the crime, and it must be a logical explanation. Foreshadowing is what makes that explanation, the outcome of your story, seem in retrospect not only plausible but inevitable. Not only should the reader have figured out this foul matter, but it *had* to end this way as surely as the last domino in a row is fated to fall once the first is toppled. Fate seemed to decree it. Your foreshadowing has created this impression. There's that "impression" business again— we know not too many things in real life fall as predictably as dominoes. But in fiction they do, so you must topple your first domino in the proper direction.

Some examples:

In my short story "The Real Shape of the Coast" written for *Ellery Queen's Mystery Magazine*, the detective, an inmate of an insane asylum, eventually reaches the inescapable conclusion that he himself is the murderer. In the first paragraph is the sentence "There are twenty of the sharp-angled buildings, each rising bricked and hard out of the sand like an undeniable fact." This isn't in any way a clue, but in a subtle way it foreshadows the ending: Eventually the detective's investigation will build what even he must acknowledge, the undeniable fact of his guilt. This domino, nudged to fall at the correct angle, was made possible because when I began the story I knew where I wanted the final domino to drop.

Consider the opening of "The Day of the Picnic" published in *Alfred Hitchcock's Mystery Magazine*:

> "South into the hot barren country of Southern California, east all the way into Arizona, that's the range of the California Condor."
>
> "Those birds fascinate you, don't they?" Judith asks. It is another of her stupid questions that are beginning to annoy me more and more.

Oh-oh. Know where this one's going? I did when I sat down to write it. I knew Judith had a date with a condor. And the reader, at least on some level, suspected it, so that when it happened it seemed all the more plausible as well as possible.

One trick in planting clues is to integrate them in the text so they seem incidental, or perhaps seem to be there for some other, obvious reason (that overlapping mentioned earlier). The reader might not find it unusual that there is a puddle in Colonel Mustard's study, for instance, if clutched in the colonel's dead hand is a plastic drinking straw. No drinking glass in the locked room, though, so maybe the reader should be wondering about *that*.

Another effective way of planting clues is through dialogue. One of your characters ponders aloud about the meaning of this or that, perhaps the fact that the straw is unbent and looks new, and has no liquid trapped in it by air pressure. A second character might explain why this is so. Perhaps the colonel used the straw only to stir his drink, not to sip it. But, as it turns out, the explanation will be inadequate. The straw had nothing to do with the puddle, which had nothing to do with anything the colonel was drinking (the colonel was using it as a bookmark, and it's had time and resilience to spring back to perfect roundness). Still, the reader will assume that he or she had the opportunity to agree with the first character. The choice was there to be made. The fact that the straw appeared unused *was* mentioned. Being fair within limits, yet deceptive, is part of the game; an obvious clue doesn't always have to be relevant to the crime itself and turn up as Exhibit A later in court.

Which brings us to yet another effective way of planting a clue: We can obscure it in a parade of possibly significant facts. The puddle and unused straw might be mentioned along with an unusual hat on a hook, an open ledger book on the colonel's desk (foreshadowing the explanation as to the use of the straw), a fishbowl containing a piranha (a possible source of the puddle, even though the fish isn't a red herring). None of these other than the puddle is important, and can later be explained away—perhaps the colonel was a cruel and stingy slumlord who kept the books and collected hats and vicious fish—but the reader is likely to fix attention on any or all of the more bizarre possible clues. Just as a solitary duck in a flock being shot at by hunters has a good chance of individual survival, your clue will probably fly by unnoticed only to touch down at the end of the story.

Foreshadowing requires equal subtlety. It should register more on the reader's subconscious than conscious mind, be more emotion than fact, so that at the end of the story the neural connections are made and possibility and plausibility merge and become indistinguishable.

A good way to foreshadow is through character. In the opening paragraph of my story "High Stakes" from *The Saint Mystery Magazine*, a man checks into a sleazy hotel with one suitcase, tips the teenage bellhop a dollar, and is sneered at. Is it a complete surprise that he's a luckless petty gambler who commands no respect, is visited by mob enforcers, and at the end of the story is treated with disdain? His stay at the hotel doesn't turn out to be a pleasant one, which seems plausible to the reader, because in the first paragraph it's been established that he's down on his luck and is the sort of person who evokes a teenage bellhop's open contempt.

Life is a random adventure, but fiction isn't. Everything on the page means something, and often more than one thing. If in the final paragraph of your story your main character, an undercover policeman, is going to be killed with his own gun, there is no problem about convincing the reader that he'd be carrying a gun. Everyone knows undercover cops usually are armed. But the ending would pack more punch if earlier in the story you described him slipping the gun into its hidden holster, or described the gun itself, or even merely established the gun was there by having him adjust it beneath his clothes as he stepped down from a bus. That way, at the end of the story, he's using a gun that has already been made real in the reader's mind, a gun the reader can see and hear when the trigger is squeezed. Since the gun is more real, when it's used the action will seem more real, and the accompanying vicarious emotion in the mind and soul of the reader will be more real. And that's what fiction's all about, engaging the reader's emotions. If you don't do that, you are simply using words to convey information, and you might as well be writing instruction manuals, where the twist ending is that the manufacturer left out a screw.

One of the main pitfalls to avoid when writing an ending is what I call The Horse Nearing the Barn Syndrome. Writing fiction is satisfying but hard work, and the tendency is to hurry things along when you know you're approaching the end of a story or novel. You want that feeling of accomplishment, and the sooner you type "The End" the sooner you'll experience it. But you haven't done your job if the reader senses this impatience in the work. The story's pacing should remain firmly under your control, so that the ending seems a natural outcome of what went before. No inconsistency should jar the reader from your fictional world, or put him or her outside the story looking in, rather than experiencing on a vicarious level what your characters are experiencing. It's comforting to know the reader's cooperating with you in achieving this mesmerizing effect. Even rooting for you. Nobody begins reading a story or novel wanting to be disappointed.

The writer's job is to create a thoroughly wrought and believable fictional world, weave a seamless illusion, and to draw the reader into that world. In most cases, it should be a world that ends not with a whimper but a bang. And the bang has to make sense.

The next time you read a story whose twist ending leaves you breathless with envy and admiration, ask yourself, Is it possible the writer isn't really all that clever, but only seems so because he or she knew from the first word where the story was going?

Of course!

CHAPTER 22

GRAY CELLS AND BLUE PENCILS

MARY SHURA CRAIG

Changes, Revisions and Self-editing

Is it really true that somewhere a writer sits down, produces a perfect first draft, collects his advance, and waits for the "best-seller" listing? If so, don't even whisper his name in my presence. I'm over age in grade to turn vindictive.

I don't even *start* by writing. To me writing is thinking written down, and thinking through a book that combines the oil and water of surprise and inevitability is hard slow work for me. I write the way I drive a car, never setting out without knowing where I am going. Since this requires knowing (and in my case, writing) the last chapter before I start the first, I have beaten my brain into pulpy submission before I even start.

And even that destination isn't enough. I have to track down and trap the voice of that story, which is neither my own nor that of the protagonist. The search for a book's voice can make the Quest for the

Holy Grail resemble a wedge of Ostertorte. But it's almost worth the angst when it finally comes. The minute I hear it and know *where* I am going, with *whom* and *why*, I'm a kid let out of school.

I get to tell a story!

Already I am deep into self-editing, changing (my mind if nothing else), and revising my original concept into something more than an amorphous image. Since the subject of this piece is self-editing, changing and revision, I need to admit right off that I sincerely enjoy the actual writing. I find it as entertaining as it is demanding and difficult. I enjoy juggling all those dozens of factors constantly. I get a kick out of commuting back and forth between written English (narrative) and spoken English (dialogue). I like the challenge of trying to maintain a solid hold on at least three frames of reference simultaneously: my own, the character's and the reader's. The process of filtering the motivations and inconsistencies of unlived lives through the screen of my own understanding startles me with new insights about both the characters and myself.

No wonder the rugs don't get vacuumed and the family dog turns sullen.

Because this part is fun, it goes swiftly. When that stack of printed sheets is at least half as high as the unanswered mail, I have a first draft. Now I face the second hard thing. I have lived that book long enough to lose touch with any other world. I am loathe to leave that safe place for the random disorder of real life.

Petulant, grumbling, disoriented, I *force* myself to put the draft away to cool off. Of course, it's perfect. (A newborn baby doesn't have warts. Only later does one notice it has Aunt Olive's despair of a nose, or Grandfather's negative chin.)

When I first learned how vital this cooling off period was, I didn't have the words to explain it. Science came to my rescue by providing a vocabulary for the phenomenon we had known instinctively. Two sides to a brain. How clever! The draft had flowed and stumbled and charged out of the right side of my brain. It had to cool off before the ruthlessly objective left side of the brain would touch it with a ten-foot cursor.

But like all tyrants, the left brain *relishes* its work. It subjects the whole to relentless scrutiny, bombarding it with questions and demands.

The Opening

Does the opening immediately engage the reader with characters, setting and action that he can't resist? Would anyone but a mother really care about the main character? Do these tattered opening pages pose the question, espouse the problem, or precipitate the crisis resolved by the ending? Is this action placed as close to the denouement of the story as possible to avoid fluttering the reader back and forth endlessly in the time travel fiction calls the flashback?

I have rewritten openings until I can recite them in my sleep. Talk about change! I lose count of the number of rewrites by the time those first few pages are simple, clear and tight enough that I can get on with the story's development.

Scenes

The reward for reworking that opening is that I get to read my book all the way through out loud to myself. I read aloud for a variety of reasons. How else can I ferret out the dialogue that can only be called unspeakable? Not every reader has mastered rapid reading. They may not move their lips but many people literally read aloud silently to themselves. Ours is a graceful language when carefully written but prose that doesn't flow irritates many readers. This can be fatal to a writer in this age of cordless channel changers.

I try to be as analytical as possible during this first reading. I don't stop when I encounter something that needs changing but simply annotate the margin. Otherwise I would get no sense of the pacing.

I am paranoid about excessive transitions. For me the power of fiction is only released in scenes which are as visual and dynamic as life.

Scenes happen somewhere. Since real-life settings register on the senses, fictional ones must too. Descriptions must be appropriate and consistent with the mind that registers them for the reader. Specificity is vital. One must name the bird, the tree, define the faint pneumatic sigh of the furnace. I prefer to limit the number of settings in a given book as stringently as possible, with the intent of rendering each one visible the first time around and registering only changes thereafter.

Totally aside from appearance and senses, places carry their own emotional weight. People tend to feel powerless in other people's space and assured in their own.

Scenes (and stories) have characters. If I prick a character, I have to see blood. Characters are well introduced much as one meets them as strangers at a cocktail party. Four factors register at once: gender, face, name and voice. The writer has the luxury of time to develop main characters through the length of the story. A succession of scenes allows the reader to assimilate the facets of the character traits that will give inevitability to the denouement and resolution.

Minor characters present different problems. The most credible protagonist in the world is diminished by interchange with cardboard dummies. This requires that I have given minor characters comprehensive treatment at their first appearance to assure that they will be both recognized and understood in subsequent encounters. Have I avoided cliché characterizations? Not all truck drivers are bawdy nor ministers simpering. Some prostitutes have hearts of base metal. But all characters either instinctively speak from the habits of their class or become wary when speaking in the company of people of other classes.

I find it helpful to know how the minor characters identify themselves to themselves. Most people run up their identity flags in the first five minutes. It's almost a parlor game.

"As a Harvard man, I . . ."

"I've never enjoyed good health."

"We men of business . . ."

"Of course I'm only a homemaker but . . ."

"I've never been one to mince words . . ."

Conversational niceties are for afternoon tea. Every word of dialogue must press the story forward, reveal character, or suggest private agendas that are pertinent to the story's development. In stories where most characters come from similar backgrounds, I have to guard against their sounding alike even though this is a phenomenon common to social groups everywhere.

I have a passion against conspicuous attributives. I believe simple ones are invisible. After all, the reader is interested principally in who is speaking and what he is saying. Such simple attributives as "said," "told him," and "replied" disappear into the woodwork. If the dialogue doesn't reveal the character's *manner* of speaking, I make a note to rewrite. Unusual attributives are like creative accounting, distracting to reader or auditor. Unless a character has more than two legs, he isn't convincing when barking, snarling or growling. (If you must have a character laugh his words, try saying the same thing out loud while bellowing or giggling. And do invite me to watch. I'm easily entertained.)

Reading the dialogue also puts me on guard against the ubiquitous adverb trailing an attributive. Better that suspicion or anger or tenderness be expressed in the dialogue itself. When worse comes to worst, there is always the option of a simple added sentence.

She narrowed her eyes as she spoke.

His flesh tightened with fury.

The Balancing Act

Do characters in conflict emerge from the scene altered in some fashion and does the scene differ from a mini-story by closing in imbalance?

Nothing moves forward without a continuous process of balance-imbalance. In order to take a step, you throw your body off its axis. The scene must open with a problem or conflict. This imbalance is righted only to be thrown into imbalance again by the intent of one of the characters — usually the loser in the encounter. The scene must close with this unfinished business clear in the reader's mind to egg him on to see what will come of this new difficulty.

All this being done, I ask myself if this scene is really necessary to the final structure of the book. If not, I have just gone through a valuable training drill and probably added a platinum star to my crown by deleting the whole bloody thing.

Checking on the scenes I've written is never enough. Hey, I'm a negotiator, not a confrontationist. I have to watch for the unwritten scene that I've tacitly promised.

If I have intimated to the reader that a scene or confrontation is coming and not produced it, I've copped out. Once you titillate your reader with a coming brouhaha, you must show him fists flying. It is dirty pool to report on who won and show the blood being mopped up. No matter how much I dislike writing some of these scenes, I am obliged to depict all action germane to the story for the reader to see, not be told about. Otherwise I break an unspoken contract between myself and the reader.

Nobody's Perfect!

By writing a draft in dead heat, one usually paces the story reasonably well. But this demanding left brain gives you signals to alert you to your lapses.

When you reach a paragraph and the Imp From Hell on your left shoulder whispers, "You know what that says," rewrite it. It's boring, too boring even for you to read and we all love our own words.

When you read a sentence that snags in your mind like a fingernail in your last pair of black nylons, rewrite it. It is awkward, or stupid, or unclear, or all of the above. (Let's hear it for the word processor, which cleans up our act by removing the onus of retyping for such modest gaucheries.)

Watch for the words you cling to as if for life. These beloved words or phrases pop up on our pages like mushrooms on a moist spring morning. Delete your darlings, or rewrite around them. You are allowed one per chapter only if the chapter is short and you can honestly report being a good sort for the previous fortnight.

I personally think that common knowledge has a lifetime batting average of about thirteen. This necessitates checking all facts relentlessly. If this involves studying beekeeping, pinning down the criminal investigation procedures of a given state, or taking a state financial officer to lunch to pick his brains about escheat law, I do it. In fairness, I'll admit that some research is more fun than others. But how could I possibly describe going upstream on a mile-wide river unless I had actually traveled there on a paddle wheel?

The bad news is that one flagrant error can undermine the credibility of the entire book; the good is that in time you become the king or queen of trivia.

No matter how careful your self-editing, you are not the final arbiter. Even when editors really like the book, they have been carefully trained to finish their sentences with "but."

The best editors, and I am happy to say I have worked with some of these, are as addicted to questions as your left brain is. A book is a forest. Editors look at trees. When asked, "Is this birch really necessary?" I often find it isn't. A good editor is *rightly* the advocate of the reader, demanding the clarity and simplicity and just good old-fashioned amusement that the ultimate consumer deserves.

The last thing you ever want to do is look at an edited manuscript or enter into an editorial consultation with your hackles up. It is almost unheard of for a responsible editor to ask for changes or request revisions that will violate the author's intent for the book. The editor is as dedicated to making this the best possible book as you are. You don't have to watch for these attempted violations. If one crops up, you will recognize it instantly. This "the place of stopping" is an invisible line that you didn't even know existed until you were asked to cross it. All manner of interior bells jangle. Fortunately, the common English word, "No" is easy to pronounce.

If that editor does not take "No" for an answer, all is not lost. If your book is all you conceived it to be, a compelling story with surprise and inevitability combined to an exhilarating froth, it will quite possibly find a home with another publisher. Worst case, the success of your next book will guarantee this one a stylish and profitable launching.

CHAPTER 23

LOCATING THE BEST AGENTS FOR YOUR WORK

SCOTT EDELSTEIN

It's quite important that you spend the necessary time selecting agents carefully; a few hours spent doing this research can save you weeks of rejection and frustration later.

No two agents are alike, and it's important to realize that an agent who may be perfect for one writer may be highly inappropriate, and quite unhelpful, for another. Agents differ widely in their temperaments and styles of doing business. Some are warm and friendly, others curt and businesslike; some are nervous and high-energy, others cool and restrained. Some keep in touch with clients primarily through phone calls, while others prefer to use the mail.

But an agent's personality and style are really secondary considerations. What you need is an agent who is honest and straightforward; who has many contacts at dozens (and ideally hundreds) of publishing houses; who regularly sells fiction books (and, if your project is a genre book, books in that genre) to major publishers; and who will work hard to sell your project. Naturally you want an agent you trust, and with whom you get along and feel comfortable; but unless that agent can actually get your project into the hands of the right people *and sell it*, he or she is not doing you much good.

Begin your search for an agent by making use of whatever personal and professional contacts you may have. Magazine and book editors in particular can often make excellent suggestions or referrals, especially genre editors.

Other writers can also make recommendations. But don't just ask them, "Who's your agent?" Probe a bit. Here are some questions you might ask: "Are you happy with the job she's done for you?" "Does she get your work out quickly, and to at least three editors at a time?" "Does she have a good instinct for finding the right editors for a project?" "Does she stick with a book until she sells it, or does she let it languish if it doesn't sell quickly?" "What are her biggest strengths and weaknesses?"

Ideally, your contacts will be able to recommend at least a couple of agents. Better still, they may also be willing to recommend you and your work to those agents. If you have no useful contacts, however, or if the contacts you have prove less than helpful, there are other effective ways to find good literary agents. One way is to work backward from the projects and writers agents represent. Make a list of some contemporary writers whose work you admire, and/or some recent fiction books you've enjoyed. If your own project is a genre book, list books and writers in that same genre; if your project is for young readers, pick writers and books appropriate for the same age group as your book. *Don't* include best-selling books or writers on this list; the agents who represent Stephen King, James Michener and Judy Blume are not likely to want to take on new clients, especially little-known ones.

Armed with your list, head for any large city or university library. Begin by collecting authors' names. If you have a title on your list for which you do not know the author, you can usually learn the name by looking up the book in the *Titles* volume of either *Books in Print* or *Paperbound Books in Print* — or, if the book you are looking up is very recent, *Forthcoming Books*. In Canada, also look at *Canadian Books in Print*.

Next, ask to see the library's biographical dictionaries of living authors. There are quite a few of these; the most common are *Contemporary Authors* (Gale Research), *Directory of American Poets and Fiction Writers* (Poets & Writers, Inc.), *International Authors and Writers Who's Who* (International Biographical Centre/Melrose Press), *Who's Who in U.S. Writers, Editors, and Poets* (December Press), and *The Writers Directory* (St. James Press). For writers of books for children and young adults, also check the multivolume work *Something About the Author* (Gale Research). Listings for many writers also appear in *Who's Who in America* (Marquis) and the regional Who's Whos such as *Who's Who in the Midwest*.

Look up the authors on your list in one or more of these directories. (Some writers will appear in several directories, some in only one or two, some in none.) Each listing will usually include the name and address of the author's agent, if he or she has one. These books should enable you to assemble a short list of agents to contact.

If this search does not lead you to information on all the authors on your list, try calling Poets & Writers, Inc., at 212-226-3586 between the hours of 11 and 3, Eastern time. Poets & Writers has a computer data bank that lists hundreds of fiction writers and, in many cases, the names and addresses of their agents.

Yet another option is to make some quick phone calls to publishers. Let's say you've had no luck tracking down the agent for hypothetical author Susan Wendt. Get a copy of one of her recent books from a bookstore or library. Turn to the copyright page. Look for the name of the original U.S. publisher of the book, and note it down. If no original or previous publisher is listed, you are probably looking at the initial edition, and should note the name and address of the publisher of the edition you're holding.

Writers living in Canada should alter this strategy a bit. See if the copyright page lists either a previous Canadian publisher or a simultaneous American publisher. If a simultaneous American press is listed, this is the firm you will need to call. If a previous Canadian publisher is noted, you'll need to locate a copy of an edition issued by that publisher, then check the copyright page of that edition for the name of the simultaneous American publisher. If no previous Canadian *and* no simultaneous American publisher is listed in an edition, you should contact the publisher of that edition. (If a publisher has both Canadian and U.S. offices, you should normally contact the U.S. office. The one notable exception to this is the paperback house PaperJacks, whose Canadian and U.S. offices operate independently.)

Your next step is to get the phone number of this publisher by calling directory assistance, or by using one of the following directories: *Literary Market Place*, *Books in Print* (Publishers volume), *Paperbound Books in Print* (Publishers volume), *Forthcoming Books*, *Writer's Market*, *Novel and Short Story Writer's Market*, and/or *Children's Writer's and Illustrator's Market*. Call the publishing house. If the press is small, ask, "Can you tell me the name of the agent who sold you _____ by Susan Wendt?" If the press is large, first ask the operator for the editorial department; then make your request of the person who answers there. Be patient; it may take a few minutes to get you the information you want, and you may be transferred once or twice. Once you get a name, you can locate the agent's address and phone number in one or more of the books listed below.

The practice of calling publishers for agents' names is neither presumptuous nor unusual, so don't be afraid to do it. If you're asked why you need the information, be honest: explain that you're a writer of book-length material seeking to locate a good agent to represent your work.

Another good way to locate agents is to read the most recent issues (ideally, at least three months) of the magazine *Publishers Weekly*, the trade journal of the book publishing industry. Each issue of *PW* is brimful of the names of agents, editors and other publishing people. When mentioning agents, *PW* often publishes the names of some of their clients, and/or describes some of the deals they've recently made. The following regular columns will be particularly helpful: Rights, Talk of the Trade, People and New Ventures.

By now you should have some names, and it's time to head for the reference books. If at this stage you've still come up with nothing, however, don't panic; the reference books will give you plenty of names (though not a great deal of information on each agent) from which to make your selections.

The following books contain good lists of literary agents in North America:

- *Guide to Literary Agents & Art/Photo Reps* (published annually).

- *Literary Agents of North America* (published every other year).

- *Literary Market Place* (published annually).

These volumes provide names, addresses, phone numbers and some general information on each agent. Areas of interest and specialization, if any, are usually indicated. Agents who handle material for film, TV and/ or stage will usually be coded with a D (for dramatic); these agents of course won't suit your purpose. Agents who handle books will be indicated with an L (for literary). Those who handle both books and dramatic material will be indicated by the letters L-D or D-L.

Some or all of these volumes may be available in your local library; most can be found in any large university library, or in the main branch of any big-city library. These books are usually kept in the reference section, often behind the reference desk.

Agents outside of the U.S. and Canada will not be listed in these books; if you are interested in contacting agents overseas, consult one or more of these reference works: *Directory of Publishing, International Literary Market Place* and *International Writer's and Artist's Yearbook*. These are often available in large libraries.

Keep in mind that bigger is not necessarily better—or worse. There are quite a few one-person literary agencies, quite a few agencies with ten or more agents on staff, and a great many in between. Some agencies of all sizes do a good job; some of all sizes leave a great deal to be desired. In fact, the same agency may have on its staff some excellent and some not-so-excellent agents. What is important is not how large an agency is, but what kind of a job the agent handling *your* work does for you.

Checklist

Ways to locate appropriate agents:

- Ask your personal and professional contacts (editors, other writers, etc.).

- List some contemporary writers whose work you admire. Using reference books and the telephone, learn the names and addresses of their agents.

- Read the Rights, Talk of the Trade, People and New Ventures columns in *Publishers Weekly*.

- Carefully read the agents' listings in reference books: *Literary Agents of North America, Literary Market Place, Novel and Short Story Writer's Market, Writer's Market*, and *Children's Writer's and Illustrator's Market*.

CHAPTER 24

DIAL M FOR MARKET

RUSSELL GALEN

Before you can market your mystery manuscript, you must figure out if it is:

• a mainstream mystery, which contains elements designed to attract readers who usually don't read mysteries, or

• a category mystery, which is the classic mystery story aimed at mystery fans.

There are many smaller divisions within the genre, and to publishers these distinctions are as important as the ones between mysteries and, say, romances or westerns. But for our purposes, we'll focus only on the divisions between category and mainstream mysteries.

The Mainstream Market

Mainstream mysteries possess elements, as important as the mystery story itself, that appeal to a wider audience. Sometimes these books aren't thought of as mysteries at all, though you and I know that's what they really are.

The elements can include humor; hipness or trendiness; a distinctive prose style or an unusually appealing or memorable lead character; and settings that give the reader an opportunity to learn about another way of life, culture or profession. The elements give the novel a larger scope by making the mystery one aspect of a plot in which the issues at stake are greater than the identity of the murderer. Or, they can turn a mystery into a mainstream thriller by concentrating on fast pacing and on creating suspense by putting main characters in jeopardy.

These mysteries are marketed to publishers like any other mainstream commercial novel . . . with a special trick. You must decide between approaching houses with mystery programs or mainstream houses that publish no category mysteries at all.

At a mystery-oriented house, you'll be talking to people who may hunger for out-of-category success, but are also proud of their association with category mysteries. Stressing the mainstream appeal of your book tactlessly, or too much, can do more harm than good. Saying "This is more than *just* a mystery," will get you kicked right out the door.

At a mainstream house, the *mystery* label can be the kiss of death. While you shouldn't insult an editor's intelligence by saying "This is not a mystery" when it clearly is, your pitch should concentrate on elements other than the mystery plot.

The Category Market

A category mystery must be offered to a house that has a mystery program. Check the bookstores and libraries, read the reviews in the Crime section of *The New York Times Book Review* and the mystery reviews in *Publishers Weekly* for a full list of which publishers have a mystery program. The publication of two or three mysteries a season signifies a house that only occasionally publishes mysteries; more than that denotes a house with a strong mystery program.

You also need to compile a list of editors who acquire mysteries; this is a specialized taste, and a submission to an editor who doesn't acquire mysteries can result in a manuscript languishing unread for months.

Don't just call the switchboard at a publishing house and ask for the mystery editor. Some houses have an editor specializing in mysteries who might not want his name given out to unknown callers. In that case you may be given a fake name or be simply brushed off. Other houses have several editors who read mysteries, and the operator may not know who to forward your call to. You can get editors' names from *Mystery Scene* and other industry newsletters, by checking the acknowledgements or dedications in recently published books, and from references such as *Writer's Market* and *Literary Market Place*. If there's a recently published mystery you admire, call the publisher and ask for the editorial department, then ask for the name of the editor who worked on that book. If you have some professional credits in the field you can also join the Mystery Writers of America (Suite 600, 236 W. 27th St., New York City 10001, tel. 212/255-7005) and get market information, as well as other useful tips.

Then determine whether the house is acquiring the type of mystery you've written. Just because you've written a mystery and sent it to the mystery editor at We Publish Lots of Mysteries Press doesn't mean you've made a smart submission. A house's interest in a particular type of mystery will fluctuate, sometimes rapidly. Check the house's recent publications of books by new authors. (Ignore the backlist of classics or longtime best-selling authors; these reflect tastes fixed long ago — not, perhaps, what the house is looking for right now.)

If you're checking paperbacks, bear in mind that some are *paperback originals* — books acquired and developed by the paperback house — and some are *reprints* picked up from a hardcover house. Paperback editors often look for different kinds of originals than they do reprints, so if you're studying the taste of a paperback house, check only its originals. Look at the copyright page (the page to the left of and facing the title page). If it's a reprint, the original hardcover house will be mentioned.

Category publishing is much more open to new, even unpublished novelists than mainstream, and mysteries are among the most open of all categories. The field has a dazzling tradition of brand-new writers selling novels to prestigious houses, and doing so without an agent. If you demonstrate a minimum amount of savvy in your submission, you can get even a top mystery editor to take a look — if you also follow these steps:

• Complete your mystery. (You'll need to send it quickly if your query attracts interest.)

• Submit to an editor who buys mysteries and who has recently bought other novels of the same type as yours.

• Send a short query consisting of one to three paragraphs describing the book and what is unique or distinctive about it; one paragraph listing your credits, if any; and one paragraph listing your personal background if there's a connection to your subject matter (you're an expert rock-climber, say, and the mystery is set in the world of rock-climbing).

• Wait for an invitation to submit the manuscript and then send it with a brief cover letter.

The same steps can be followed to query agents. Many mystery markets, unlike most mainstream markets, accept unagented submissions, if the above procedures are followed. Having an agent puts you at a great advantage, but if you're having trouble finding one, you may be better off going directly to editors. Then have an agent negotiate the contract after you've found a publisher. (Few will turn you down at that point.)

Making the Deal

A first mystery won't bring much money; the key to making money in this genre is to develop an audience by producing new books regularly. This is not a field in which it makes sense to dabble. An editor won't be interested if he or she suspects you're not planning to continue writing mysteries regularly. If you have a track record in another field, be sure to say that your hope and intention is to stay with mysteries.

Should you seek a hardcover or paperback deal?

Hardcovers are more likely to be reviewed and to sell to book clubs. If all goes well, they can produce more money in the long run. You'll receive royalties on the hardcover, a share of the book club income, and, if the hardcover publisher sells reprint rights to a paperback publisher, a share of that income as well. But your hardcover might never become a paperback; those houses are plenty busy with their own new authors and buy only a fraction of those published by hardcover houses. In that case, your hardcover sales of 4,000 to 5,000 copies won't be enough to spread any serious word of mouth and build your audience for the future.

A paperback original, however, might sell 30,000 copies or more, and then you'll have 30,000 people across the country telling their friends about you.

Another advantage of paperback originals is that 100 percent of the royalties go into your pocket, and if the book stays in print for many years, that can add up. If the book is first sold to hardcover, the hardcover house will keep 50 percent of your paperback money for as long as the paperback stays in print.

Both hardcover and paperback have their advantages. Anyway, it's more likely you're mainly worried about getting a sale. If you have a book suitable for Scribner's or St. Martin's (which are hardcover houses), try them first and don't worry about whether you'd be better off with a paperback original. If you think a paperback house like Pocket or Bantam is your best shot, worry about getting into hardcover later. All the paperback mystery lines are divisions of larger companies with hardcover imprints, and if your paperbacks sell well, eventually your new books could be published by the hardcover imprint. (In that kind of deal, where the hardcover and paperback are published by the same conglomerate, you get the best of both by keeping 100 percent of hardcover and paperback royalties.)

Breaking and Entering

Plotting mysteries is like composing music in sonata form or poetry in rhyming meter: you have limitless freedom in some areas, but also must follow certain rules. If a mystery doesn't contain a murder in its first third (in most cases it should come as early as possible), and if the identity of the murderer isn't revealed as a result of an investigation, it's not a mystery. It may be a crime novel or a caper novel or a thriller, but it's not a mystery.

But to break in, a new writer must offer something beyond the basic mystery plot. A new writer *must* offer something new, and the pressure to do so has produced a number of exciting new writers with unique, individual voices and themes in recent years. They range from brilliant exponents of the classic category mystery to experimentalists and trend-setters.

Variation within restriction is the rule of thumb for a new writer trying to break in. If you ignore the restrictions, you risk creating an unpublishable mystery. If you fail to create an original and unique variation, you'll have a book that, whatever its sheer quality, can't compete against the hundreds of other new mysteries being published every year.

Before composing a new mystery, try this test. See if you can, in 50 words or less, summarize the distinctive qualities of this story. If you can do it in a single sentence, so much the better. Keep that summary around, because this—the novel's "hook"—will be the basis of your query letter when the time comes to market the manuscript. In one form or another it could end up in the catalog and jacket copy of the printed book, and be the main factor in bookstores', libraries' and readers' decisions to investigate the book further despite your unknown byline.

The variation can be anything so long as it's something that might sound like fun and can be said about no book but yours. Something general, such as "What's special about this book is its humor" or "The writing is exceptionally good" or "It's unusually fast-paced and suspenseful," isn't enough to make a place for an unknown author: there are plenty of established authors already out there who are as funny, distinguished or suspenseful as you. Buyers will choose them over you every time.

(Also, if you put *too* much emphasis on other elements, what you wind up with is a gimmick, something so outrageously clever and odd that it puts off traditional mystery fans, who are a rather conservative audience.)

The mere existence of a fascinating variation is no magic key to salability. It's simply the ingredient that must be added to the traditional strengths that have given mystery writing a century of unbroken popularity and made it the preeminent field for the discovery of new writers.

Surviving in the Magazine Market.

To sell short stories, follow the advice of writer Jo Gilbert:

> Finding a magazine to publish your short mystery could be the easiest case you ever solve — if you're willing to do the detective work needed to analyze your manuscript and the market, searching for clues to a perfectly molded submission.
>
> One thing to remember when marketing your mystery is that, generally, your story should be just that . . . a mystery. No mainstream stories with just a hint of crime. No romances on the side. Because of space availability, editors want short, but fully developed, category mysteries.
>
> These simple rules will also help:
>
> • Study market information. Reading the market listings will tell you the length requirements. (Many magazines average between 2,000 and 4,000 words per story. Most magazines require those numbers for a maximum length; a few list 10,000 as a word maximum and even fewer go higher.) You will also find out what types of mysteries are wanted and what the magazine's submission standards are. Don't send the complete manuscript if editors prefer to see a query or outline.
>
> For information on specific markets, consult *Writer's Market*, *Novel & Short Story Writer's Market*, monthly market listings in *Writer's Digest*, and Mystery Writers of America newsletters.

• Once you've identified your suspects, request the writer's guidelines for additional information. Include a self-addressed, stamped envelope (SASE) with your request. The guidelines will usually go into detail regarding submission standards, word length, audience profile and so forth.

• Prepare a readable manuscript. Your submission may not be read if the editor has to use a magnifying glass. The black ink should be *black* and on white paper. On the first page, type your personal identification information — name, address, telephone number — in the upper left-hand corner. In the opposite corner, put the approximate word count (round it to the nearest hundred).

Double-space with one-inch margins all around. If you're sending photocopies, make sure they're clear, too. (Photocopies *are* acceptable; never send your only copy of a story.)

• Most important, *always* include a SASE with your query or manuscript. You'll look more professional and editors will be more likely to give you a quicker response. If your submission doesn't draw a reply by the magazine's stated response time, wait an additional two weeks, and then send a brief note (with a SASE) asking for an update. If you have not received a response within three weeks after sending your note, call the editorial office.

Picking up these simple — yet important — clues could put you on the trail to getting your short mystery published.

CHAPTER 25

THE MYSTERY NOVEL FROM THE EDITOR'S POINT OF VIEW

RUTH CAVIN

Lurking under that title is another, more straightforward one. In a paraphrase of Papa Freud, it asks "What does an editor want?"

That's an easy one. What editors want, of course, is a wonderful crime novel that will get terrific reviews, sell thousands and thousands of copies, and make everyone rich and happy.

That's not very helpful, however.

Unfortunately, there is no step-by-step program that, if followed faithfully, will culminate in a finished work that every editor is guaranteed to love and want to publish. All I can do here is describe to you what an acceptable, buyable, publishable mystery looks like to me.

Manuscripts from agents and authors come to me on an average of about five a week, and that is the rate for most of my colleagues as well. The editor must do a million other things involved in getting out a list and still find time to consider all those submissions. We simply can't afford to plough through ninety very ordinary pages because there might be a real gem on page ninety-one.

So you must learn how to Grab The Editor. Unfortunately, authors too often misunderstand the nature of what grabs an editor. It's *not* having bloody mayhem on the first page. Nor is it that (perhaps unconscious) scam that puts a dark, ominous prologue in front of what is a perfectly pedestrian story.

No.

What I want is a beginning that excites my interest so that I want to read on, and that shows me that the author has a unique and personal way of seeing things and writing about them. Most of the many manuscripts that come across my desk are pretty good. But they are, many of them, ordinary—there is nothing special about them. By "special," I don't mean two-headed serial killers or neckties that strangle people of their own accord (I had a proposal like that once, honest). I mean "special" in the sense that the author is able to make the story stand out from the crowd because of a fresh approach, a noticing eye, an able pen. (An able word processor? Sounds funny.)

Before you rise in rage and get me blackballed by Mystery Writers of America, let me be quick to say that I don't mean I read only the first paragraph of a submission. I give it much more of a chance than that. But over the years, I've found that the unusual, the extraordinary, signals itself pretty clearly very early on. And the unusual and the extraordinary is what this editor wants.

If *you* had forty or fifty manuscripts waiting to be read and chronic guilt about not being able to get to them—or through them—fast enough, which of the opening paragraphs below would encourage *you* to take the manuscript home to read that evening?

> They say three's a crowd and I had a good idea Mrs. Phillips had called me because there was a woman somewhere she wanted out of the picture. Usually I wouldn't touch a divorce case while wearing surgical gloves, but the D.A. had lifted my license and my piece and it was either this or take back the neat Liz Claiborne I'd sent home that morning. A colored man [!] in a uniform opened the guard gate for me, and by the looks of the place, I'd have a full resort wardrobe by the first of the year.

> Trouble. The feeling struck Frank Limosin the instant he saw the girl. She was sitting on the rear deck of a fiery red Trans Am that stood slumped on a flat rear tire by the side of the road in the hot empty desert. The warning of trouble

persisted, telling him more than he wanted to know about how old and fusty he'd become, but also it had something to do with the $77,000 in unmarked bills he had stashed behind a false back in one of the camper's cabinets.

The first excerpt tells you there's a wisecracking female private eye who is going to a rich woman's house and is assuming she will be asked to snoop on an erring husband. The second tells you that a man, not young, with $77,000 of somehow ill-gotten money is driving a camper through the desert and has encountered a young girl with an expensive and conspicuous car that is disabled. That she's not doing anything about her problem and doesn't seem very upset about it tells us something about her right away.

The first paragraph is like heaven knows how many other books about wisecracking private eyes, rich female clients and cases that may turn out not to be routine. The second tells you a great deal that's new and interesting and promises more. Both manuscripts fulfilled the expectations of their opening paragraphs. I bought the second: Robert Leininger's *Killing Sukie Flood*.

Occasionally an agent or author will ask me whether I have any "guidelines" to give writers who aspire to be published by St. Martin's. Yes, indeed, I do. Here they are:

1. Double-space your manuscript.

2. Use one side of the paper only.

3. Number the pages consecutively, not chapter by chapter.

4. If the submission is directly from the author, enclose return postage.

Those are my guidelines.

What did you expect? "The detective should be between twenty-seven and forty years old?" "The murder should happen on page fifty-two?" Uh-uh.

I don't want mystery novels that are written to a formula. The good mystery novel is, first of all, a good novel. It is a mystery because it is built around a crime and (with variations) the search for the perpetrator of that crime. I want a solid story with a life of its own, not a written-by-the-numbers tale that seems to have bored its author as much as it will bore me.

The most important element of the mystery novel, to my mind, is *character*. I want to believe in the people of the story. I can't really care what is going to happen if it's going to happen to some two-dimensional puppets, paper dolls stuck together with Elmer's glue and pushed through a series of actions. Readers of mysteries must be able to involve themselves in the story to the extent that it matters very much what happens to the *people* in it. Develop your characters and you'll find that they do half your work for you in return.

(It's true that the more sophisticated the readers, the more depth they demand in the characters; there are those whose needs are satisfied with approximate facsimiles — recognizable stereotypes whose reality they can take for granted. Not me. I want real people.)

Some of the suggestions here might help you give me what I want:

• In a play (or movie or TV drama) the writer has only three ways to "describe" the people in it:

By what the character says.

By what the character does.

By what others in the work say about the character.

You, however, can tell the reader anything you want to: what kind of person the character is, his or her weaknesses or strengths, whatever. There's nothing wrong with taking advantage of that freedom, but the more you can work within a playwright's restrictions, *showing* rather than *telling*, the more effective your character will be.

• Don't regard your characters as being there simply to act out your story. Look on them as real people. Imagine yourself an actor preparing to play the different parts and do some real thinking about each one. What is the person's history? How would that character react to situations other than those in the story? What are his or her fears? Fantasies? Hopes? Even though these enriching details never appear in the finished manuscript, they will have a positive effect on what you do put down on paper.

• Observe everyone — relatives, friends, Romans, passengers on the bus. Borrow mannerisms from real life — *but only those that tell us something about the character you have created.*

I've said this next so often that it's now a cliché that I have a patent on. If the characters are believable, the background and atmosphere real and interesting, and the writing smooth and accurate (I'll give you my definition of "accurate" writing later on), I'm not going to worry too much about plot problems unless the basic premise is irretrievably flawed.

They're usually quite fixable. If the plot is neat and logical and the characters are wooden, the prose is clunky, the atmosphere nonexistent—then there's little, if any, hope of salvaging the story.

You notice I don't say "Plot doesn't matter." It matters very much in a mystery. Regardless of how far today's mysteries have departed from the strict puzzle and become bona fide novels, the story is still vital. What I do say is "It can be fixed."

Plot generates its cousin, suspense. It is suspense that keeps you reading and wanting to know what is going to happen.

What creates suspense is a threat. There must be the prospect of something really bad happening *unless* . . . Unless the crime is solved. Unless something intervenes between the villain and his or her intention. This is what gives your sleuth a solid motive for pursuing the matter, and you need that motivation. I see too many manuscripts that don't give the detective any reason but curiosity for trying to solve the case. I call that the Nancy Drew Syndrome. Adult readers have gone beyond Nancy Drew; curiosity is not enough. (It's pretty silly, too.) You need the threat of another murder, or of having someone we like suspected of the crime or arrested for it. Or a sympathetic character marked for extermination by the criminal. A police officer must have some stronger motivation than just the requirements of his or her job: rivalry in the department, the desire to "show" a superior, a fixation that justice has miscarried, a question of career advancement or failure.

If you read a lot, and read different kinds of writers, notice what you're reading, and do a good bit of writing on your own, chances are you'll develop your own prose style. You won't do it by trying to copy a writer you admire; you'll do it, in part, by noticing what other writers do *not* do as well as what they do.

A while back I mentioned accurate writing. I'm not talking here about accuracy of content; I assume you know you should get your facts straight. I'm talking about saying exactly what you mean to say and not some approximation of it.

"He looked up to see the back of silky brown hair, gently curling three inches below the collar of her blouse."

"She turned and walked out of the room. He watched her narrow hips glide away."

And this real dilly:

"The pleasant demeanor melted from his face and it became a mask of vicious hate."

Obviously, "He" didn't see the back of silky brown *hair*, he saw the back of a head covered with silky brown hair. As "She had her back to him; her silky brown hair curled gently below the collar of her blouse."

Nor did her narrow hips glide away all by themselves. Instead, "He watched her narrow hips as she glided away." (Although I'd prefer that only someone on skis or ice skates glided.)

The last one is too extreme to talk about.

Those are rather startlingly clear examples of inaccurate writing. Watch out for more subtle ones in your own work.

Notice details and use them — but use them wisely. Details that tell the reader something about the character or the situation, or that enhance the atmosphere of the story, are the secret of vivid writing. Details just sprinkled about for no particular reason except that some book on writing tells you to use details are a liability.

"He turned toward the left and rested his arm on the back of the bench."

Who cares? Get on with the story.

Have faith in yourself and your readers. They'll understand what you're saying very well without your having to spell everything out for them. I see this kind of thing so often; it pains me to see it:

"He got up from the couch, walked to the TV and switched it off. Then he went over to the kitchen. He opened the door and went up to the table where Jane was making sandwiches."

I made that one up, but it's hardly an exaggeration of what I come across. In fact, come to think of it, it's no exaggeration at all.

"He turned off the television. In the kitchen, he found Jane making sandwiches."

That's all you need. Say what you have to say as clearly and straight-forwardly as possible and your own style will emerge and keep refining.

Don't misunderstand me. I'm not advocating that everyone go in for sparse, Hemingway-like prose. If your sentence is thirty words long, just be sure that every one of those thirty words is there because it has something specific to do, and that the total effect is one of total communication.

Where's the action?

I'm not looking for a crap game, I'm talking about a sense of place. Your story is not happening in a vacuum; I want details that make the setting real to me — details that evoke the locale: the weather, the buildings, the interior, whatever. Places have characteristics of their own, and a writer should be able to convey that.

Take advantage of our collective semiconsciousness when you can:

"Clean up on aisle eight." Ted flipped off the intercom

and sighed. It was bad. Salad oil. As spills went, it was right up there with mayonnaise and peanut butter. . . . Nobody seemed to be hustling over there with a mop, but a little old lady with a walker, listing slightly because of a heavy nylon shopping bag hanging from one handle, was making steady progress toward the oil slick.

The author has never mentioned the word "supermarket," but we know damn well that that's where this is going on. Everyone in the United States knows that salad oil spilled in aisle eight says "supermarket." This bit of narrative economy is from K.K. Beck's, *The Corpse in the Cornflakes*.

It's a real plus if you can use some special knowledge you have in your story. Readers love it—they're getting a bonus. Gideon Oliver's physical anthropology. Lovejoy's phenomenal knowledge of antiques. The Navajo lore from Joe Leaphorn and Jim Chee. If you can work it into your story as an integral part of the action and not just something that's stuck in awkwardly, go for it.

Finally, I have to go all psychic on you. An editor will leap for joy to find a writer with what we call "voice." It's what we always hope for in a manuscript; it's what we find to a greater or lesser degree in the better ones; occasionally it will be present in such force as to knock us back on our heels. It's a quality in the writing that's hard to define, but when you come across it, you *know*. It is clear and unequivocal and unique to that writer, setting him or her apart from all others. From two different authors:

> The morning sun has ever been a provider of comfort; one of its nicest attributes is that there is always enough to go around. The same morning sun that had highlighted the bat's blood on Gad's feet, that had touched Max as he sat down to a morning meal near a British Rail station just west of London, spread itself effortlessly and settled its mantle across Sparrow House.
>
> Julia, lying on her back . . . opened her eyes to it. She lay awhile with tears on her lashes, following the movement of ray and mote across the painted ceiling, registering the warmth without noticing, her mind reading back into the lost hours, trying with the futile desperation of waking to recapture the night.

They looked up and watched the garbage truck come lumbering up the block. Mrs. Dixon next door stretched her terry bathrobe around herself one extra time, slammed down the can lid, and waddled briskly back inside her house. No garbagemen were going to see *her* front without a sturdy brassiere. Of that they could be sure. Some things, Claire smiled, never changed. Then a decrepit Plymouth rattled down the broken street from Park Lane South and turned left onto Myrtle. And back they fell to sleep.

The first vivid panorama is from Deborah Grabien's *Plainsong*; the second is from Mary Anne Kelly's *Park Lane South*. So now I've come full circle, haven't I, with my dissertation on "voice." I said something very much like that when I was talking about openings — about Grabbing The Editor. I can't tell you how to get it; it comes of writing a lot and loving to write — *having* to write. Of being self-critical, of knowing what you want to have happen in your work, of reading, reading, reading. And of being lucky enough to have what the Wagnerian tenor, Lauritz Melchior, once called "a little touch of God's finger." Old unbelievers like me call it less poetically "a special talent."

There it is — this editor's "want list." I would guess it's very much like the want lists of most editors. Recently one of my first-time authors called me when he got his manuscript with all my editorial notes on it. This man has a great pair of detectives, fine secondary characters, a solid familiarity with an interesting milieu, and a good ear for dialogue. His prose, however, overall, was still rough. It needed, shall we say, polishing.

I polished. I cut out all the "he walked to the television" and that mark of so many new writers, the "thens" — "He got up, then left." "She spotted her father, then waved." I cut lines and lines of deadwood detail. What was left was fine, and the author, far from taking umbrage, was delighted.

"I learned more about writing in a week from your criticisms than I learned in two years from books," said he. I was grateful, but it's a dubious compliment, really. I'm not all that sure you can learn from books, where there's no one going over your own material with a fresh eye. (I'm a great believer in writing groups for that reason.) One learns to write by writing, but it's true that someone can steer you in the direction you should take, rather than your having to flounder about at the crossroads. I hope I've done that, if only a very little bit. Once your feet are on the road, it's up to you. Happy journey!

PART 3

SPECIALTIES

CHAPTER 26

WRITING MYSTERIES FOR YOUNG READERS

JOAN LOWERY NIXON

D o you remember the excitement you felt when you read your first
mystery novel? The overwhelming awe that such a marvelous form
of storytelling had been invented? You shivered, you jumped at a sudden
noise in the hall, you moved to sit close to your father, but you kept
reading as though you were under a spell, hoping that no one would
remember it was past your bedtime. As soon as you finished reading the
last page of the book you immediately searched for another mystery to
read. And another. And another. You were hooked.

Juvenile mystery writers often find their books on lists for reluctant
readers; teachers and librarians will tell them how kids who won't read
anything else devour mysteries; and the young people themselves will
write letters such as these: "I hate to read, but I read one of your mysteries, and now I want to read everything you've ever written." "I'm fifteen.
I'm in the ninth grade. I never read a book in my life until I read your
mystery novel, and I loved it. Our librarian promised to give me some of
your other books."

Why do kids of all ages love mysteries so much? Why do they demand them and buy them and read them in such quantities that almost all publishers of juvenile books carry one or more mysteries on each list?

Reader Identification

Children of elementary school age are great at identifying wholeheartedly with the main characters of the books they read. When young readers dive into mystery stories they *become* the main characters — the persons who are brave enough to tackle something strange or mysterious or frightening — and through these vicarious experiences they grow a little in independence. They prove their bravery. They tackle a situation far beyond their own back-and-forth-to-school routines, and they conquer it. Bring on the next challenge! A mysterious box? A ghost in the attic? A mummy in the basement? Just watch how fast the reader becomes involved in the next story and — with a little help from the main character — again faces danger and solves the mystery!

Character rapport is the key here. The main character of any mystery story should be likable, with a few welcome faults (such as procrastination, forgetting homework, losing patience with a pesty little brother), which call on the sympathy of young readers. Characters' actions should be well motivated, consistent and believable so that readers can easily step into their shoes. But "can" is not enough. Readers must care enough about the main characters so that they *want* to step into those shoes.

Because children like to feel older, never younger, it helps, too, to make your main character as old as those in the upper age group who will be reading the stories. Publishers classify reading groups as six to nine, seven to eleven, eight to twelve, nine to thirteen, and young adult: ages ten and up.

To aid reader identification, most books for young people are written in single viewpoint, although multiple viewpoint can be used for young adult readers.

Gripping Beginnings

Young people from primary grades through the teen years are demanding readers. They will pick up a book, read the first few paragraphs — or even sentences — and if they aren't immediately captured they'll put down the book and reach for another. It's up to the juvenile mystery author to begin his story with intrigue, action or suspense. The opening sentence should grab readers; the next few paragraphs should be fascinating enough to ensure that this book is going to be read.

While many mystery novels for adults start with a leisurely pace, taking time to offer a sense of place, set the scene, and introduce many of the characters before the events leading to the mystery begin to take shape, mystery novels for young readers immediately bring in the main character and toss him into the action.

For very young readers the opening sentences can be just slightly scary, with the realization that something is mysteriously out of order. Mystery stories for children in the primary grades could be called *puzzle mysteries*, and these puzzles fit into the reader's frame of reference. Perhaps something is missing. It might have been mysteriously switched for something else. It could be that something out of the ordinary has suddenly appeared. Maybe there's a shadow in the hall or a sound that can't be explained.

Humor is frequently used in books for beginning readers because it's a nice balance to tension; it creates the valleys between the peaks of suspense.

But readers in the eight to twelve and young adult categories want a full-fledged mystery, and they want to be shocked into tension, suspense and fear right from the start. This means that after the opening scene that thrusts them into the mystery, flashbacks containing background information will often have to be woven into the story.

Flashbacks should contain only the most necessary information. It's often surprising how much background material really isn't important and can be left out. That which is important can be woven in through dialogue or through the main character's thoughts.

Original Ideas

With the exception of some mass-market series with single plot lines, today's successful juvenile mysteries deal with unusual, original situations, many of them relying on current problems that touch young lives.

The teenaged main character in Norma Fox Mazer's *Taking Terri Mueller* (Avon) is shocked and horrified when she begins to realize that she is a kidnapped child—kidnapped when she was only five by her father who had lost custody after a bitter divorce. Even though Terri's father has always said that her mother had died when she was five, Terri is sure that he had lied, and she sets about trying to find her mother.

Lois Duncan's main character, April, in *Don't Look Behind You* (Delacorte) is a teenaged girl whose father is a government witness with his life in danger; and the entire family must "disappear" with new identities.

April is told she can't say goodbye to her friends and that she will not even be able to get in touch with them after the flight; but, brokenhearted at the thought of never seeing her boyfriend again, she breaks the rules, and a hit man from the crime syndicate is soon on the family's trail.

Betty Ren Wright deals with a haunted dollhouse in *The Dollhouse Murders* (Holiday House), as her main character, Amy, discovers that the dollhouse dolls are trying to give her the clues she needs to solve a murder that took place on the property many years ago.

Susan Beth Pfeffer writes of a family in which the younger brother mysteriously disappears without a clue in *The Year Without Michael* (Bantam). And in my mystery novel, *The Other Side of Dark* (Delacorte/Dell), a teenaged girl wakes from a four-year comatose state to discover not only that she is seventeen, instead of thirteen, but that she is also the only eyewitness who can identify the person who murdered her mother.

Demanding Plots

Plot and character development are so tightly interwoven that they grow together as the idea takes shape. The direction the story follows depends upon the main character's actions and reactions because the story belongs to the main character.

The successful juvenile mystery novel has two interrelated story lines: The main character has a personal problem that must be solved, and the main character has a mystery to solve.

Each of the mystery novels above contains this dual story line. In *Taking Terri Mueller* the mystery is complex. Terri must discover her true identity and, without her father's knowledge, try to find her mother. Terri's emotions play a large part in this story: the torment she feels when she is sure her father has lied to her and is responsible for this strange, ever-moving life in which she can't put down roots or make real friends, the love-hate anguish at knowing her father has kept her from her mother all these years; and the fear that if she does contact her mother, her father will be put into prison. Terri has to handle her own feelings and come to a sensible course of action as well as solve the mystery.

April's identity and life-style are suddenly snatched away in *Don't Look Behind You*. Against her will even her name has been changed. Everything about her life seems to vary at the whim of the government agent in charge of her family; and she has to deal with the anger she feels toward the government, her father, her mother, and—eventually—even herself.

Amy, in *The Dollhouse Murders*, must deal with her own feelings of rejection by her mother, her jealousy of the attention her younger sister, Louann, is receiving, and her resentment of having to watch over this retarded sister.

As *The Year Without Michael* develops, Jody is devastated. She watches her family life crumble and those she loves split farther and farther apart. Desperately, she tries to bring them together as she aches with loneliness for the little brother she may never see again.

Stacy struggles to make up the four lost years of her life in *The Other Side of Dark*, at the same time mourning the death of her mother and trying to come to terms with the problems her eyewitness status is causing her family.

Anger, hatred, resentment, loss, fury, the desperate need to be loved — main characters in mysteries for young people have to learn to handle their personal problems as well as solve mysteries.

Suspense!

The mystery plot for today's impatient young readers is fast-paced and filled with action. Writers should pull out all the stops and use any and every technique for establishing suspense. These are a few of the ways in which this can be done:

1. Use the description of the setting to help create and maintain suspense.

2. Your main character makes a mistake, which is obvious to readers, and takes a wrong course of action.

3. Time is rapidly running out. Will the main character make it?

4. The main character needs some information, and the person who has it is tantalizingly slow to come forward with it. The delay tantalizes readers, too.

5. Suspicion can be thrown on someone the main character has trusted. Maybe it's just the reader who becomes suspicious, and the main character is innocently unaware. When will the main character wake up and discover the danger she's in?

6. Unexpected surprises can make a sudden shift in the story's direction. Was it a wrong turn or a right one? Read and find out.

7. Readers are made aware that something dangerous or frightening will happen to the main character, but they don't know when it will take place.

8. Peculiar characters may fit only certain stories, but when they do appear they add suspense.

9. Chapters should end with dangling questions, creating such suspenseful curiosity that young readers can't put the book down and *must* go on to the next chapter.

Show, Don't Tell

Young readers have grown up with the highly visual drama presented in movies and television, and they think visually. A ninth-grade girl recently wrote to me, "I got really excited when suddenly Marti turned around and saw Emmet. I jumped because in my mind I was picturing the story; and if it were a movie, the volume of the music would have suddenly gotten louder and everyone would have jumped."

Writing can be every bit as visual as its media counterparts when it appeals to the imagination. Sensory perception and strong action verbs help writing become vivid and visual, and the frequent use of dialogue pulls readers into the story. If a story in a mystery novel moves from scene to scene, then narration will be minimal.

Be Sure of the Facts

It all comes down to respect for your readers. If you care about them, you'll double-check every fact. Be familiar with the background in your story. Write only about places in which you've lived or have traveled for the purpose of doing research.

If your story involves any type of police procedural, talk to someone at your local police headquarters. Make sure you've got it right. If you're including job information—anything from working in a fast-food place, an attorney's office or an under-the-city sewer—do your research well, because there are kids out there who'll know if you're right or wrong, and they write letters. Do they ever! If you're right, they'll praise you, and if you're wrong, they'll let you know. If you lose their trust you've lost them as readers.

Of course, it's a foregone conclusion that as a good mystery writer you'll never withhold a clue or hold back information that's necessary to solve the crime.

Your mysteries can follow the path of detection or the back alleys of psychological suspense. They can reach afield to combine with science fiction, the western, the historical, the romance and the humor novel. They can open horizons and provide new directions. And because each year new crops of kids discover mystery novels and make them their reading favorites, juvenile mysteries will continue to rank high on publishers' lists.

CHAPTER 27

THE JOYS AND CHALLENGES OF THE SHORT STORY

EDWARD D. HOCH

The Joys

All right, why do I write short stories? Why does anyone, for that matter, in today's market? I've had well-known authors tell me that if they thought of an idea good enough for a short story, they'd expand it into a novel. I've had well-known agents tell me if they're taking an editor to lunch they want to be selling him a novel, not a short story.

There's no hiding the fact that the immediate financial gain from a novel is usually about ten times greater than that from a short story. Unless you're selling to markets like *Playboy* or *Redbook* or *Woman's Day*, short story payments generally range from three to ten cents a word, with some borderline publications still offering the 1920s pulp rate of a penny a word. Occasionally an original anthology built around a highly marketable theme might offer more, but that's about it as far as the initial publication goes.

However, there is money to be made in short stories over the long haul. I have dozens that have been more profitable for me than the handful of novels I published twenty years ago. While a book publisher can tie up most rights, taking a cut from reprint editions and sometimes even from foreign sales and film rights, magazine publishers generally buy only first North American serial rights, occasionally with an option on first anthology rights as well. In most cases the writer is free to sell onetime nonexclusive rights to a story anywhere in the world—a weekly newspaper in England, a radio station in Switzerland, or a mystery magazine in Japan. In this country there are frequent anthologies, compilations of short stories on audiotape, and even appearances in textbooks. (One of my early stories has been reprinted more than thirty times in textbooks for high school and junior high students.) If you're lucky, a single television sale can bring more than the advance on a novel.

But only a fool would write short stories solely for money. There has to be something more to it than that. In my case I am blessed (or cursed) with the ability to think up plots faster and more easily than I can fully develop them and set them down on paper. The novels I've attempted have dragged on for months in the writing, while all the time other ideas were crowding their way into my mind. I wanted to be done with that novel and on to the next story. The stories I write now, generally ranging from 5,000 to 7,000 words, can be finished and polished in two weeks or less. That's just about right for me, and I'm usually started on the next story before the latest is in the mail.

Graham Greene observed that an author is the same person when he starts and finishes a short story, whereas a novel that takes a year or more to write can find him a different person, with different views on some of the fundamental concepts of the book. A short story gives the writer the exhilaration of completing a job, and you can experience this exhilaration two or three times a month! On a more practical note, if your short story doesn't happen to sell to the first or second editor to see it, there's not the frustration of having wasted months or a year of your life. Already you can be working on the next story while seeking other markets for the reject. And short story editors usually decide on submissions within a few weeks, not the months required for manuscripts of novels.

Short stories alone may never make a writer famous, unless his name is Poe, but they can bring in a good income over the years, provide a nice change of pace for novelists, and offer the beginning writer a perfect opportunity to hone his craft before tackling a longer work.

Getting Started With Characters and Setting

The first thing for a writer in our field to decide is whether he wants to write a mystery or a suspense story. Either way, he needs an opening that will grab the reader. If that opening can also introduce a character and establish the setting, so much the better. An opening line that did all three was Graham Greene's lead-in to his novel *Brighton Rock*: "Hale knew, before he had been in Brighton three hours, that they meant to murder him."

I tried to do something similar with the opening of my short story "Murder of a Gypsy King," which begins: "On the long, lonely highway into Bucharest that sunny August afternoon, Jennifer Beatty suddenly changed her mind." In each of these examples, the reader is introduced to an important character and given the setting for the story. There is also a question implicit in these openings. Why do "they" want to murder Hale, and why did Jennifer Beatty change her mind? These questions are designed to hook the reader, to keep him or her reading to find the answers.

If your story is set in the past, or in an unfamiliar city, some research will be necessary. I have built mysteries around Jumbo, the circus elephant, and the Wright Brothers' first flight, among other things. Both required considerable research for just a few sentences of facts and descriptions. For a story about America's first centennial on July 4, 1876, I consulted a microfilm copy of the *New York Times* for that date.

My stories about British cipher expert Jeffrey Rand and Romanian Gypsy Michael Vlado are often set in European cities. The Rand stories venture even further, and I was pleased when a reader complimented me on the authentic Hong Kong background in one of them. I'd never visited Hong Kong, but reading a couple of recent books gave me all the background I needed. I find two sources to be invaluable for research on unfamiliar cities. One is a street map of the city, and another is photographs, particularly street scenes. Most guidebooks can furnish these. Mentioning streets your characters travel, even if only a passing reference, adds greatly to the realism of the story. Other important facts that guidebooks can supply are the temperatures and rainfall for different seasons. All the world isn't like home. To have a sunny day during some city's rainy season, or to forget that seasons are reversed in the southern hemisphere, can be fatal errors.

Many mystery writers spend a great deal of time researching police procedure. I have never found this to be necessary in short stories with their limited space, because such procedures can vary from city to city. My Captain Leopold stories, semi-procedurals, are set in a fictive city, so I feel the police there can follow their own rules within certain limits.

Within the close confines of the short story, character, plot and setting are in a constant battle for space. If the plot and setting are to be developed, it's almost always characterization that suffers. With a series detective it's possible to overcome this problem over the space of several stories, giving the reader bits of character development as the series progresses. But what about a non-series mystery, or a suspense story?

Some characters in mystery stories often seem to exist in a vacuum. Their past is never mentioned, and the readers know nothing about them except for their actions during the time frame of the story. This particular approach isn't really wrong, and with the right sort of character it can sometimes add a certain mystique to the story. But to get the reader fully involved with your character it's much better to offer bits and pieces of the past — childhood, love affairs, military service, earlier cases. Occasionally, there's a good reason for not revealing a character's past — at least not until the end of the story. One of my own non-series stories deals with a wandering stranger who arrives in a small town and solves a murder. At the end of the story the reader learns that the stranger himself is an escaped killer.

Plots and Clues

With a series character, the plot often flows out of the character himself. A private eye investigates certain types of cases. A police detective usually has other types. No private detective would be hired to investigate a murder or a bank robbery, unless the authorities had failed in their task or some unusual elements were present. Private detectives more often encounter murder while searching for a missing person or doing some sort of security work. In period pieces the private eye can still be seen gathering evidence for a divorce case, though the easing of divorce laws have made such investigations fairly uncommon today. The so-called amateur detective, of course, can be found investigating just about anything, and no one worries about all the murders that seem to crowd into his life. In the thirteen years he's lived in the New England town of Northmont, my detective Dr. Sam Hawthorne has encountered no less than forty impossible crimes and locked room murders — an improbable number by any standards.

Writers often get their plots from the pages of the daily newspaper, although I prefer to build plots around some odd fact or unusual setting that I come upon. Occasionally I might even get a plot idea from a motion picture or a novel, usually by thinking of ways in which I could have improved upon the original author. I've just completed a story about a young woman who comes to New York in 1953 and takes a job working for three men with diverse professions who share office space. The idea grew out of the memory of a novel I read as a teenager, coupled with a Broadway play I saw just a few months ago.

If your story is to be straight suspense, possibly with a twist at the end, there need be no concern with clues. Even if the story is a mystery, there's no commandment that says the author must play fair with the reader and allow him or her to solve the mystery along with the detective. Arthur Conan Doyle and Sherlock Holmes often withheld information from the reader. Chesterton's Father Brown was better, but it was not until writers like Agatha Christie and Ellery Queen that fair play became a necessity.

I think many of today's writers view the placing of good clues as hard work that can be dispensed with quite easily. Admittedly, today's short story cannot contain the sort of involved explanations that Ellery Queen used to indulge in during the 1930s, but it can still have one or two good clues.

The easiest (laziest) sort of clue is the false statement by a suspect, or a statement that reveals knowledge the suspect shouldn't have had. For example, a man learns that his wife has been murdered and he immediately asks, "Do you know who shot her?" without having been told the cause of death. Other clues can involve some physical trait, such as the killer's being color-blind, or right- or left-handed.

The dying message clue was used extensively in Ellery Queen's later short stories, but in using a dying message the writer should try to make the circumstances believable. There has to be a reason why the dying person would scrawl some obscure message rather than just write the killer's name. I once did a story about stolen icons in which the second victim was found dead of a bullet wound in his room, having lived long enough to print the word ICON. This man had committed the first murder himself. Wounded by a police bullet, he lived long enough to return to his room and start to write out a confession. He died before he could finish the words I CONFESS.

The killer's identity is often arrived at by a process of elimination. Out of five suspects, perhaps only three had the physical strength for the crime. Only two of those had the knowledge that would give them a motive. And only one had access to the weapon that was used. Other clues can involve physical forces such as gravity. In one of Isaac Asimov's science fiction detective stories, the killer has badly misjudged the distance he can throw an object, falling far short of his mark. The detective rightly concludes that the killer was more familiar with a world where the force of gravity was much less, and he arrests the only one of the suspects who has just returned from a lengthy stay on the moon.

Perhaps the best clues of all are ones that make good use of the detective's abilities, either because of special training or inherent knowledge. In one of the best Kinsey Millhone short stories, Sue Grafton's private eye spots a clue involving a woman's diaphragm — the sort of clue a female sleuth would spot more quickly than a male.

Solutions and Conclusions

I think it was John Dickson Carr who once stated that the perfect locked room mystery would have a solution that could be given in one sentence. That's true of any mystery, but unfortunately if you want to play fair with the reader you're probably going to need more space than that to point out your clues and explain the reasoning behind them. My stories generally run from twenty to twenty-five pages in manuscript, and I feel I can use two of those pages for the solution. There are times when even that seems long, though. Certainly Carr's one-sentence windup is the goal to strive for.

It's not always necessary to surprise the reader with every story. Sometimes the plot is such that a more conventional ending is called for. With just about every story I write there comes a time when I sit back and think about the ending I'm heading for. I ask myself if it's an ending that really satisfies me as a reader. With new writers, especially, an ending should be one that sticks in the reader's mind, that he or she remembers the next time they encounter your name on the contents page.

I think the first story by Edgar Allan Poe that I ever read was "The Pit and the Pendulum" in one of my school textbooks. I read those last four sentences: "An outstretched arm caught my own as I fell, fainting, into the abyss. It was that of General Lasalle. The French army had entered Toledo. The Inquisition was in the hands of its enemies." I read them, and I remembered their impact. I sought out every story of Poe's that I could find.

It was an ending that completely satisfied the reader, as I'm sure it satisfied Poe. We all can't be Poe, but if we satisfy ourselves there's a good chance we'll satisfy the reader as well.

Selling Your Story

These days, with so few markets for short mystery fiction, there's no sure rule for success. Happily, both of the nationally distributed mystery magazines, *Ellery Queen's Mystery Magazine* and *Alfred Hitchcock's Mystery Magazine*, are especially hospitable to stories by new writers. Beyond that, there are an increasing number of original anthologies being published — though these are not often open to the beginning writer. Some of the mystery fan publications like *The Armchair Detective* and *Mystery Scene* are now publishing a limited amount of fiction. Their rates are not as high as the professional magazines, but they should be considered by someone just breaking into the field.

If a story doesn't sell to the first few editors who see it, there's a tendency to change and revise it, especially if one editor has offered some concrete objections to certain plot points. My own feeling is that if you believe in a story you should stick with it, revising it only if a contract is offered. My Edgar-winning story "The Oblong Room" was rejected a few times before finding a home in *The Saint Magazine*. Only one of my eight stories that have appeared on American television sold to the first editor who saw it. The other seven had all been rejected at least once.

As I indicated earlier, literary agents aren't too interested in handling short stories these days, unless it's for an established client who's also a novelist. I've been fortunate in having many of my overseas sales handled by an agent who specializes in such things, but for this country I'm pretty much on my own.

Still, it's a pretty good feeling when those letters of acceptance arrive in the mail. It's not even that bad when the rejections come in, because there's always the possibility of selling to a new market and reaching a whole new audience.

A Reference List for Mystery Writers
Bruce Cassiday

Arena, Jay M., and Richard H. Drew, eds. *Poisoning: Toxicology, Symptoms, Treatments*. C.C. Thomas, 1986.

Bartollas, Clemens, and Simon Dinitz. *Introduction to Criminology*. Harper & Row, 1988.

Berrey, Lester V., and Melvin Van Den Bark. *The American Thesaurus of Slang*. Crowell, 1945.

Block, Lawrence. *Writing the Novel: From Plot to Print*. Writer's Digest, 1985.

Blye, Irwin, and Ardy Frieberg. *Secrets of a Private Eye; Or How to Be Your Own Private Investigator*. Henry Holt, 1987.

Bond, Raymond T. *Handbook for Poisoners*. Collier Books, 1962.

Brean, Herbert, ed. *The Mystery Writer's Handbook*. Harper & Brothers, 1956.

Budd, Elaine. *13 Mistresses of Murder*. Ungar, 1986.

Burack, Sylvia K., ed. *Writing Mystery and Crime Fiction*. The Writer, 1985.

Dulles, Allen. *The Craft of Intelligence*. Harper & Row, 1963.

Farago, Ladislas. *The Game of the Foxes*. McKay, 1972.

Freeman, Lucy, ed. *The Murder Mystique: Crime Writers on Their Art*. Ungar, 1982.

Geherin, David. *The American Private Eye: The Image in Fiction*. Ungar, 1985.

Goldin, Hyman E., Frank O'Leary, and Morris Lipsius. *Dictionary of American Underworld Lingo*. Twayne, 1950.

Gonzales, Thomas A., Morgan Vance, Milton Helpern, and Charles J. Umberger. *Legal Medicine: Pathology and Toxicology*. Appleton-Century-Crofts, 1954.

Haycraft, Howard. *The Art of the Mystery Story*. Carroll & Graf, 1983.

Haycraft, Howard. *Murder for Pleasure*. Carroll & Graf, 1984.

Hutchinson, Maxwell. *Poisoner's Handbook*. Loompanics, 1988.

Kahn, David. *The Code-Breakers*. Macmillan, 1967.

Kamisar, Yale. *Modern Criminal Procedure* (American Casebook Series). West Publishing Co., 1986.

McCormick, Mona. *The New York Times Guide to Reference Materials*. Popular Library, 1971.

Melling, John Kennedy. *The Crime Writers' Practical Handbook of Technical Information*. The Crime Writers' Association, 1989.

Newton, Michael. *Armed and Dangerous*. Writer's Digest, 1990.

Nicholson, Margaret. *A Dictionary of American-English Usage, Based on Fowler's Modern English Usage*. Oxford University Press, 1957.

Norville, Barbara. *Writing the Modern Mystery*. Writer's Digest, 1968.

OCork, Shannon. *How to Write Mysteries*. Writer's Digest, 1989.

Partridge, Eric. *A Dictionary of Slang and Unconventional English*. Macmillan, 1970.

Reddy, Maureen T. *Sisters in Crime: Feminism and the Crime Novel*. Ungar, 1988.

Reik, Theodor. *The Unknown Murderer*. International Universities Press, 1978.

Reilly, John. *Twentieth Century Crime and Mystery Writers*. St. Martin's, 1985.

Roth, Martin. *The Writer's Complete Crime Reference Book*. Writer's Digest, 1990.

Schultz, Donald, and Samuel Scheer. *Crime Scene Investigation*. Prentice-Hall, 1977.

Smyth, Frank. *Cause of Death: The Story of Forensic Science*. Van Nostrand Reinhold, 1980.

Steinbrunner, Chris, Charles Shibuk, Otto Penzler, Marvin Lachman, and Francis M. Nevins, Jr. *Detectionary*. Hammermill Paper Co., 1971.

Steinbrunner, Chris, Otto Penzler, Marvin Lachman, and Charles Shibuk. *Encyclopedia of Mystery and Detection*. McGraw-Hill, 1976.

Stevens, Serita Deborah with Anne Klarner. *Deadly Doses*. Writer's Digest, 1990.

Stone, Evan, and Hugh Johnson, eds. *Forensic Medicine* (Criminal Law Library). Pergamon, 1987.

Strunk, William, Jr., and E.B. White. *Elements of Style*. Macmillan, 1979.

Symons, Julian. *Bloody Murder: From the Detective Story to the Crime Novel*. Penguin, 1984.

Treat, Lawrence, ed. *Mystery Writer's Handbook*. Writer's Digest, 1976.

Vandiver, James V. *Criminal Investigation: A Guide to Technique and Solution*. Scarecrow, 1983.

Wentworth, Arnold, and Stuart Berg Flexner. *Dictionary of American Slang*. Crowell, 1960.

Wambaugh, Joseph. *Lines and Shadows*. Bantam, 1985.

Whitney, Phyllis. *Guide to Fiction Writing*. The Writer, 1982.

Wilson, Colin, and Patricia Pitman. *Encyclopaedia of Murder*. Pan Books, 1984.

Woeller, Waltraud, and Bruce Cassiday. *The Literature of Crime and Detection: An Illustrated History From Antiquity to the Present*. Ungar, 1988.

Tools of the Trade

Chapman, Robert L. *Roget's International Thesaurus*. Crowell, 1977.

Grosvenor, Melville Bell, and James M. Darley, eds. *National Geographic Atlas of the World*. National Geographic Society, 1963.

Levey, Judith H., and Agnes Greenhall, eds. *The Concise Columbia Encyclopedia*. Avon, 1983.

Webster's Ninth New Collegiate Dictionary. Merriam-Webster, 1983.

Author Biographies

Lawrence Block

Lawrence Block has written more than thirty novels, mostly mystery and suspense, and has won many awards, including the Edgar, the Nero, and the Shamus. He is a member of the International Narcotics Enforcement Officers Association and the International Association for the Study of Organized Crime. He lives in New York with his wife Lynne, who is a descendent of Edgar Allan Poe.

Rex Burns

Rex Burns's series characters include Denver homicide detective Gabe Wager and private eye Devlin Kirk. *Body Guard* is the latest Devlin Kirk yarn. The ninth Gabe Wager novel will be out in 1992. Burns also writes under the pen-name "Tom Sehler." He lives in Boulder, Colorado, and teaches at the University of Colorado at Denver.

Max Byrd

Max Byrd is the author of five novels, most recently *Target of Opportunity* and *Fuse Time*. He was educated at Harvard and now makes his home in northern California where he teaches writing at the University of California, Davis. He also teaches every year at the Squaw Valley Community of Writers.

Robert Campbell

Robert Campbell is the author of the Edgar Award winning *Junkyard Dog*, the first book in the Jimmy Flannery Mystery Series. He also writes the La-La Land Series that features Whistler. The latest book in that series is *Sweet La-La Land*.

P.M. Carlson

P.M. Carlson writes mysteries featuring the bright, lively, and sometimes outrageous Maggie Ryan, who is statistician, mom, and sleuth. *Murder Unrenovated* was a finalist for both Anthony and Macavity awards. *Murder in the Dog Days* and *Murder Misread* are the latest in the series.

Bruce Cassiday

Bruce Cassiday's most recent mystery novel is *Murder Game*. He is currently at work on *Modern Mystery, Science Fiction, and Fantasy Writers* for Ungar's Library of Literary Criticism. Other critical works are *Roots of Detection* and *The Literature of Crime and Detection*, along with contributions to *The New Bedside, Bathtub & Armchair Companion to Agatha Christie*. He has written radio mystery dramas, short stories, a long-running series featuring federal operative Johnny Blood, and more than twenty mystery novels.

Ruth Cavin

Ruth Cavin is a senior editor and associate publisher under the Thomas Dunne imprint at St. Martin's Press where she publishes, among other works, a large number of mysteries. Previous to that, she was Mystery Editor at Walker and Company. In 1988 she was honored to receive the Ellery Queen Award for contributions to the mystery genre from Mystery Writers of America.

George C. Chesbro

George C. Chesbro is the author of seventeen novels (the latest is *The Language of Cannibals*), three dozen short stories, poems, articles, and a sound filmstrip series for handicapped children and adults. He is the creator of the Mongo Mystery Series. He occasionally lectures on the business of writing, and is a member of the national board of directors of Mystery Writers of America.

Mary Shura Craig

Mary Shura Craig has authored more than twenty-five best-selling children's books, numerous adult mysteries, several short stories, and poetry for both popular and scholarly magazines. Some of her writing is under psuedonyms. Mary was a past president of Mystery Writer's of America-Midwest, and is credited with beginning their annual workshop on techniques in mystery writing. She was also past national president of Mystery Writer's of America.

Scott Edelstein

Scott Edelstein is a full-time freelance writer whose stories and articles have appeared in a wide variety of magazines, from *Ellery Queen's Mystery Magazine* to *Glamour* to *Writer's Digest*. His most recent books include *The Writer's Book of Checklists* and *Manuscript Submission*, both from Writer's Digest Books. He lives in Minneapolis.

Aaron Elkins

Edgar-winner Aaron Elkins is an ex-professor who began writing mysteries ten years ago. His two series feature anthropologist-detective Gideon Oliver and art curator-sleuth Chris Norgren. They have been made into a major television series, have been Book of the Month Club selections, and have been published in England, Japan, Sweden, Switzerland, and Finland. His latest book is *Make No Bones*, a Gideon Oliver novel.

Russell Galen

Russell Galen is vice president of the Scott Meredith Literary Agency. The agency represents more than fifty mystery writers, which includes best-selling authors and award winners. Russell also writes "New York Overheard," a marketing advice column for *Writer's Digest* magazine.

Sue Grafton

Sue Grafton entered the mystery field in 1982 with the publication of *'A' Is for Alibi*, which introduced female hard-boiled private investigator, Kinsey Millhone, operating out of the fictional town of Santa Teresa, California. *'B' Is for Burglar* followed in 1985 and since then, she has added a novel a year (including *'C' Is for Corpse*, *'D' Is for Deadbeat*, *'E' Is for Evidence*, *'F' Is for Fugitive*, *'G' Is for Gumshoe*, and *'H' Is for Homicide*) in what are now referred to as 'the alphabet mysteries.' At the current rate, she will complete the series in the year 2008.

Bill Granger

Bill Granger has written twenty-four books. He won the Edgar Award from the Mystery Writers of America for *Public Murders* and is the author of the November Man Series, including *League of Terror* and *The Man Who Heard Too Much*. He has been a journalist for the Chicago Sun-Times, United Press International, and the Chicago Tribune. He lives in Chicago and writes a regular column for *The Chicago Tribune Magazine*.

Jeremiah Healy

Jeremiah Healy is a professor at the New England School of Law in Boston. His first novel, *Blunt Darts*, was selected by the *New York Times* as one of the seven best mysteries of 1984. His second book, *The Staked Goat*, received the Shamus Award for the Best Private-Eye Novel of 1986. A four-time Shamus nominee, Healy's later novels include *So Like Sleep*, *Swan Dive*, and his most recent, *Yesterday's News*.

Tony Hillerman

Tony Hillerman is best known for his novels set on the Navajo Reservation involving the Navajo Tribal Police. He was elected Grand Master of Crime Writing by Mystery Writers of America in 1991, and won the 1974 Edgar for *Dance Hall of the Dead*. He was proclaimed "Special Friend of the Dineh" by the Navajo Tribe. Other honors include the "Anthropology in the Media" award of the American Anthropological Association, and a Special Award of the U.S. Department of Interior for publicizing problems involving public lands. He lives in Albuquerque, New Mexico.

Edward D. Hoch

Edward D. Hoch, past president of the Mystery Writers of America, is the author of more than seven hundred published short stories and fourteen novels and story collections. He has had a story in every issue of *Ellery Queen's Mystery Magazine* since May 1973, and since 1976 he has edited *The Year's Best Mystery and Suspense Stories*, a yearly anthology. Hoch and his wife Patricia live in Rochester, NY.

Faye Kellerman and Jonathan Kellerman

Faye Kellerman's most recent novel is *Day of Atonement*. She has written four other novels, including an acclaimed historical mystery, *The Quality of Mercy*. She is currently at work on a new Peter Decker/Rina Lazarus mystery. Edgar-winner Jonathan Kellerman's novels include *When the Bough Breaks, Blood Test, Over the Edge, The Butcher's Theater, Silent Partner*, and *Time Bomb*. Like his detective hero, Kellerman was trained as a clinical psychologist specializing in children. He is the author of two volumes on psychology and one book for children. The Kellermans live in Los Angeles with their three children.

Dick Lochte

Dick Lochte's debut novel, *Sleeping Dog*, won the Nero Wolfe Award for Best Novel and was nominated for the Mystery Writers of America Edgar Award and the Private-Eye Writers Shamus Award. His new novel, *The Burial Society*, will be published in 1992. An award-winning theater critic for *Los Angeles Magazine*, he has written for both feature films and television. His articles and essays have appeared in numerous magazines and newspapers. He resides alternately in Southern California and New Orleans, Louisiana.

John Lutz

John Lutz has two current private-eye series, the Nudger novels, set in Saint Louis, and the Carver novels, set in Florida. Also he writes short stories and non-series suspense novels. His most current novel is *SWF Seeks Same*. He's received the Edgar Award (1986), two Shamus awards (1982, 1988), and the Polar Festival Award for best French language mystery short story collection of 1988.

Gregory Mcdonald

Gregory Mcdonald wrote his first novel, *Running Scared*, when he was twenty-three. He won the Edgar Allan Poe Award for a novel, *Fletch*, in 1975, and its sequel, *Confess, Fletch*, in 1977. He has written a total of twelve mysteries, nine Fletch novels and three Flynn novels. In 1986, he was president of The Mystery Writers of America. Greg has received several humanitarian awards, one of which is the 1990 Roger Williams Straus Award from the National Conference of Christians and Jews. Greg lives on a cattle farm in Campbellsville, Tennessee.

Warren Murphy and Molly Cochran

Winners of three Edgars, the husband-wife (should we say wife-husband?) writing team of Murphy and Cochran have co-authored more than a dozen books including *Grandmaster*, *The Temple Dogs*, and most recently, *The Forever King*, which will be out in 1992. Murphy, who created the long-running Destroyer and Trace series, is also a screenwriter. They live with their young son, Devin, in a historic manor house outside Bethlehem, Pennsylvania.

Joan Lowery Nixon

Joan Lowery Nixon has authored over eighty books, the most recent of which is the young adult mystery, *A Candidate for Murder*. She has won three Edgars from Mystery Writers of America and many children's choice awards throughout the United States. She is listed in *Contemporary Authors of Children's Literature*; *Something About the Author*, volume 44; *Something About the Author Autobiographies*, volume 9; and *Who's Who in America*, volume 46.

Sara Paretsky

Sara Paretsky is the founder of Sisters In Crime and the author of six novels featuring private investigator V.I. Warshaski: *Indemnity Only*, *Deadlock*, *Killing Orders*, *Bitter Medicine*, *Blood Shot*, and *Burn Marks*. She lives in Chicago with her husband, physics professor Courtenay Wright, and their golden retriever.

Nancy Pickard

Nancy Pickard is the creator of the Jenny Cain series of amateur sleuth mysteries and of short stories of psychological suspense. She's the winner of the Agatha, Anthony, Macavity, and American Mystery awards and an Edgar Award nominee. Pickard is a former president of Sisters in Crime and a member of the board of directors of the Mystery Writers of America. Her novels include *Generous Death*, *Bum Steer*, and *I. O. U.*.

Sandra Scoppettone

Writing as Jack Early, she was given a Mystery Writer's of America Edgar nomination in the 1984 best first mystery category for *A Creative Kind of Killer*, and by Private-Eye Writers of America for a Shamus, which she won. The following year, as Scoppettone, she was nominated for an Edgar in the YA division. Her latest mystery, *Everything You Have Is Mine*, is under her own name and introduces a lesbian private eye.

Julie Smith

Julie Smith's *New Orleans Mourning* won the Edgar Allen Poe Award from the Mystery Writers of America for best novel of 1990. Police officer Skip Langdon, introduced in that book, returns in Smith's newest, *The Axeman's Jazz*. Smith also writes about two San Francisco sleuths — lawyer Rebecca Schwartz and Paul McDonald, and ex-reporter who writes mysteries. Schwartz appears in *Death Turns a Trick*, *The Sourdough Wars*, *Tourist Trap*, and *Dead in the Water*, McDonald in *True-Life Adventure* and *Huckleberry Fiend*. Like McDonald, Smith is a former reporter.

Marilyn Wallace

Marilyn Wallace's novels include *A Case of Loyalties* (Mystery Readers International Macavity winner, 1986), *Primary Target* (a 1989 Anthony Award nominee), *A Single Stone*, and *So Shall Ye Reap* (which will be published in 1992). Editor of the five-volume *Sisters in Crime* anthology series and co-editor with Robert J. Randisi of *Deadly Allies*, she is also a past president of the Northern California chapter of Mystery Writers of America.

Phyllis A. Whitney

Phyllis A. Whitney has long been a best-seller in the mystery-suspense field. She received the Grand Master Award from Mystery Writers of

America in 1988. Also an Agatha Award from Malice Domestic in 1990. Both were given for lifetime achievement. For many years she taught writing at New York University, and has published two books on writing: *Guide to Fiction Writing*, and *Writing Juvenile Stories and Novels*.

Carolyn Wheat

Carolyn Wheat's first mystery, *Dead Man's Thoughts*, was nominated for an Edgar for Best First Mystery of 1983. It introduced Brooklyn defense lawyer Cassandra Jameson. She has a short story in *A Woman's Eye*, edited by Sara Paretsky, and another in *Sisters In Crime*, volume 4. Ms. Wheat teaches mystery writing at The New School in New York.

INDEX

Permissions Acknowledgments

OTHER BOOKS OF INTEREST

Annual Market Books
  Artist's Market, edited by Lauri Miller $21.95
  Children's Writer's & Illustrator's Market, edited by Lisa Carpenter (paper) $17.95
  Guide to Literary Agents & Art/Photo Reps, edited by Robin Gee $15.95
  Humor & Cartoon Markets, edited by Bob Staake (paper) $16.95
  Novel & Short Story Writer's Market, edited by Robin Gee (paper) $18.95
  Photographer's Market, edited by Sam Marshall $21.95
  Poet's Market, by Judson Jerome $19.95
  Songwriter's Market, edited by Brian Rushing $19.95
  Writer's Market, edited by Mark Kissling $25.95
General Writing Books
  Annable's Treasury of Literary Teasers, by H.D. Annable (paper) $10.95
  Beginning Writer's Answer Book, edited by Kirk Polking (paper) $13.95
  Discovering the Writer Within, by Bruce Ballenger & Barry Lane $17.95
  Getting the Words Right: How to Rewrite, Edit and Revise, by Theodore A. Rees Cheney (paper) $12.95
  How to Write a Book Proposal, by Michael Larsen (paper) $10.95
  Just Open a Vein, edited by William Brohaugh $15.95
  Knowing Where to Look: The Ultimate Guide to Research, by Lois Horowitz (paper) $16.95
  Make Your Words Work, by Gary Provost $17.95
  Pinckert's Practical Grammar, by Robert C. Pinckert (paper) $11.95
  12 Keys to Writing Books That Sell, by Kathleen Krull (paper) $12.95
  The 29 Most Common Writing Mistakes & How to Avoid Them, by Judy Delton (paper) $9.95
  The Wordwatcher's Guide to Good Writing & Grammar, by Morton S. Freeman (paper) $15.95
  Word Processing Secrets for Writers, by Michael A. Banks & Ansen Dibell (paper) $14.95
  The Writer's Book of Checklists, by Scott Edelstein $16.95
  The Writer's Digest Guide to Manuscript Formats, by Buchman & Groves $18.95
  The Writer's Essential Desk Reference, edited by Glenda Neff $19.95
Nonfiction Writing
  The Complete Guide to Writing Biographies, by Ted Schwarz $19.95
  Creative Conversations: The Writer's Guide to Conducting Interviews, by Michael Schumacher $16.95
  How to Do Leaflets, Newsletters, & Newspapers, by Nancy Brigham (paper) $14.95
  How to Sell Every Magazine Article You Write, by Lisa Collier Cool (paper) $11.95
  How to Write Irresistible Query Letters, by Lisa Collier Cool (paper) $10.95
  The Writer's Digest Handbook of Magazine Article Writing, edited by Jean M. Fredette (paper) $11.95
Fiction Writing
  The Art & Craft of Novel Writing, by Oakley Hall $17.95
  Best Stories from New Writers, edited by Linda Sanders $16.95
  Characters & Viewpoint, by Orson Scott Card $13.95
  The Complete Guide to Writing Fiction, by Barnaby Conrad $17.95
  Cosmic Critiques: How & Why 10 Science Fiction Stories Work, edited by Asimov & Greenberg (paper) $12.95
  Creating Characters: How to Build Story People, by Dwight V. Swain $16.95
  Creating Short Fiction, by Damon Knight (paper) $10.95
  Dialogue, by Lewis Turco $13.95
  The Fiction Writer's Silent Partner, by Martin Roth $19.95
  Handbook of Short Story Writing: Vol. I, by Dickson and Smythe (paper) $10.95
  Handbook of Short Story Writing: Vol. II, edited by Jean Fredette (paper) $12.95
  How to Write & Sell Your First Novel, by Collier & Leighton (paper) $12.95
  Manuscript Submission, by Scott Edelstein $13.95
  Mastering Fiction Writing, by Kit Reed $18.95

Plot, by Ansen Dibell $13.95
Spider Spin Me a Web: Lawrence Block on Writing Fiction, by Lawrence Block $16.95
Theme & Strategy, by Ronald B. Tobias $13.95
Writing the Novel: From Plot to Print, by Lawrence Block (paper) $11.95
Special Interest Writing Books
Armed & Dangerous: A Writer's Guide to Weapons, by Michael Newton (paper) $14.95
The Children's Picture Book: How to Write It, How to Sell It, by Ellen E.M. Roberts (paper) $19.95
The Complete Book of Feature Writing, by Leonard Witt $18.95
Creating Poetry, by John Drury $18.95
Deadly Doses: A Writer's Guide to Poisons, by Serita Deborah Stevens with Anne Klarner (paper) $16.95
Editing Your Newsletter, by Mark Beach (paper) $18.50
A Guide to Travel Writing & Photography, by Ann & Carl Purcell (paper) $22.95
Hillary Waugh's Guide to Mysteries & Mystery Writing, by Hillary Waugh $19.95
How to Pitch & Sell Your TV Script, by David Silver $17.95
How to Write Action/Adventure Novels, by Michael Newton $13.95
How to Write & Sell True Crime, by Gary Provost $17.95
How to Write Horror Fiction, by William F. Nolan $15.95
How to Write Mysteries, by Shannon OCork $13.95
How to Write Romances, by Phyllis Taylor Pianka $13.95
How to Write Science Fiction & Fantasy, by Orson Scott Card $13.95
How to Write Tales of Horror, Fantasy & Science Fiction, edited by J.N. Williamson (paper) $12.95
How to Write the Story of Your Life, by Frank P. Thomas (paper) $11.95
How to Write Western Novels, by Matt Braun $13.95
The Magazine Article: How To Think It, Plan It, Write It, by Peter Jacobi $17.95
Mystery Writer's Handbook, by The Mystery Writers of America (paper) $11.95
The Poet's Handbook, by Judson Jerome (paper) $11.95
Successful Scriptwriting, by Jurgen Wolff & Kerry Cox (paper) $14.95
The Writer's Complete Crime Reference Book, by Martin Roth $19.95
The Writer's Guide to Conquering the Magazine Market, by Connie Emerson $17.95
Writing for Children & Teenagers, 3rd Edition, by Lee Wyndham & Arnold Madison (paper) $12.95
Writing the Modern Mystery, by Barbara Norville (paper) $12.95
The Writing Business
A Beginner's Guide to Getting Published, edited by Kirk Polking (paper) $11.95
The Complete Guide to Self-Publishing, by Tom & Marilyn Ross (paper) $16.95
How to Write with a Collaborator, by Hal Bennett with Michael Larsen $11.95
How You Can Make $25,000 a Year Writing, by Nancy Edmonds Hanson (paper) $12.95
Writer's Guide to Self-Promotion & Publicity, by Elane Feldman $16.95
A Writer's Guide to Contract Negotiations, by Richard Balkin (paper) $11.95
Writing A to Z, edited by Kirk Polking $22.95

To order directly from the publisher, include $3.00 postage and handling for 1 book and $1.00 for each additional book. Allow 30 days for delivery.

Writer's Digest Books
1507 Dana Avenue, Cincinnati, Ohio 45207
Credit card orders call TOLL-FREE
1-800-289-0963
Prices subject to change without notice.

Write to this same address for information on *Writer's Digest* magazine, *Story* magazine, Writer's Digest Book Club, Writer's Digest School, and Writer's Digest Criticism Service.